C000182782

Satan's Little White Lie

by William Schnoebelen

***Front cover design
by Dean Roberts***

Library of congress Card Catalog No: 90-82581
ISBN: 0-937958-34-4

179/D

Published by Chick Publications, Inc.
P.O. Box 3500, Ontario, CA 91761-1100 USA
Tel: (909) 987-0771 • Fax: (909) 941-8128

Printed in the United States of America

Outside the U.S. call for a distributor nearest you or see our entire listing on the internet at: **www.chick.com/distrib.asp**

HOW TO REACH US:
Complete list of Chick titles on World Wide Web: www.chick.com
By E-Mail: postmaster@chick.com

Contents

Foreward

Many people are writing books these days about the occult. Many of them have been deeply involved themselves. Having found the Lord Jesus Christ and been set free, they leap to the call of reaching back to help others find freedom from that same sphere of darkness. Bill Schnoebelen is one of those people. He was in that darkness and was set free by the power of the cross!

However, the scriptures also warn us to be cautious with new Christians, that in time, each man's heart will be made known. We have seen more than one babe in the gospel burn before our very eyes as they stepped into battle with the powers and principalities of darkness.

We are also warned to lay hands on no one suddenly (I Tim. 5:22) no matter how exciting someone's testimony and background may seem. That scriptural warning holds doubly true for anyone coming out of Witchcraft!

I asked that I be allowed to write the Foreward because it is important for you to know that Bill Schnoebelen passes the test of close spiritual scrutiny.

I first came into contact with Bill over five years ago, as he took his first steps into the Christian community. He was definitely on fire for the Lord and wanted to charge forth into the ministry.

I held back for almost two years of close communication before I invited him to come and speak to a national conference on Mormonism which we hosted. There I was able to meet him face to face and discuss his interest in full time service. I decided to offer him a position on staff at Saints Alive and bring him under the covering of our spiritual authority.

Bill has now been in service at Saints Alive for over three years. He works with me on a daily basis. His office is next to my own. I have read every one of the thousands of counseling letters he has sent to people struggling with every kind of occult darkness. I have listened to hundreds of his phone conversations, listened in to scores of personal counseling sessions, and many of his public ministries.

I know the man. I have never heard him utter a word of advice that didn't point to Calvary. I have never seen a letter leave his desk that didn't offer the reader the hope of the Cross. I have seen hundreds of besieged people walk out of our offices set free from darkness and delivered from the hands of the destroyer. Bill has personally led more people to Jesus than I could even count.

I watched this book as it was written. I watched Bill labor over certain areas in it. I read the manuscript drafts. We discussed the many questions it raises. I reviewed the final manuscript before it was sent to the publisher. I am excited about this book. I am excited about the things it will accomplish in exposing the satanic evil behind Wicca.

I earnestly recommend the book and Bill Schnoebelen to you, confidently taking full spiritual responsibility for that statement. The book is of a quality that speaks for itself.

I wanted you to know that the man who wrote it is a proven, mature Christian who is correctly submitted in the body of Christ, and a man you can trust. I can truly say of Bill, that he walks "worthy of the Lord unto all pleasing, being fruitful in every good work, and increasing in the knowledge of God." (Col. 1:10)

Your brother in Christ,

Ed Decker
President
Saints Alive in Jesus

Introduction

I was a witch! I was a **sold-out**, **goddess-worshipping** witch! When my "lady" and I chipped the ice out of a stream in the middle of Iowa wilderness to bathe and then celebrate the March equinox naked under the stars, we were totally consumed with zeal for the Wicca. We drove 170 miles one way every weekend to teach classes in Wicca in a car with a bumper sticker which said *"In Goddess We Trust!"*

We were kicked out of almost every apartment we tried to rent for wild circle dances and burning frankincense; and we had a firebomb thrown into one temple because we dared to publicly proclaim the goddess!

Wicca is one of the more seductive deceptions that Satan has come up with.[1] It is the contemporary name for the cult of so-called "white" witchcraft or Neo-Paganism, which has been enjoying a renaissance in the United States.

It claims to be a "back to nature" religion which worships the sky and earth, and thus has attracted many adherents among those sympathetic to environmental and ecology issues. Yet, for all its charm and nostalgic fantasy, Wicca drew me into the deepest quagmire of satanic evil imaginable.

Almost everything we did back then raised eyebrows. Regrettably, we see people today doing things openly that we had to do in secret. We see books that used to only be available in dark, musty occult bookstores now being sold openly in shopping malls. The meditation practices we taught in secret witchcraft circles are now being taught in "respectable" churches.

Naturally, we believed we were doing good. I was a sincere devotee of the chief deity of Wicca, the Great Mother. At first I believed the rites we did were for the benefit of humanity and the earth itself. I also believed what I was told: that there was a **profound** difference between the Wicca and those called satanists or devil-worshipers.

I thought that the whole meaning of Wicca was beneficial rituals to nature deities like Pan, Diana or Cernunnos; and of course rites of passage and initiation. I stood, blindfolded, naked and bound at the edge of the Circle "which is placed between the worlds." I heard the words of the Great Mother and felt the prick of the swordpoint challenging my courage. I was anointed as a "Priest of the Goddess" and learned her secret name. I gave my life to her service.

I truly believed that she was the One "who was with me from the beginning, and who was attained at the end of desire." I walked the earth and felt her a living, breathing thing; and I worshiped her as "Holy Mother Earth."

It took me sixteen years of ardent devotion to her and the Craft to find out that I was terribly wrong. I had to learn the hard way that my only hope for true spiritual fulfillment in life was Jesus Christ!

I finally learned in the most graphic fashion imaginable that the difference between witchcraft or Wicca and satanism is actually non-existent. To be sure, an anthropologist or sociologist of religion might find them different, but such distinctions mean little when you are gambling with the eternal fate of your own immortal soul.

The actual spiritual difference between Wicca and satanism might best be illustrated this way: Practicing Wicca is like having a hand-grenade blow up in your face, in terms of the spiritual impact. Practicing satanism is like having an neutron bomb detonate in your face. The difference is there and discernable, but it is still an utter disaster for you, either way.

In eternal perspective, the disaster of Wicca is altogether real and no less dangerous than that neutron bomb.

Why Should YOU Believe This Warning?

Before we discuss this subject, allow me to give my credentials. I was initiated into the *Alexandrian Wicca* on Imbolc, February 2, 1973 and made a High Priest and Magus in September of the same year. That summer my lady and I were also promoted to the High Priestly rank in the *Druidic Craft of the Wise*. We also helped establish a *Church of All Worlds* "nest" in Milwaukee and studied under Gavin and Yvonne Frost and their *Church and School of Wicca*.

Wicca has many "denominations" or traditions. Some are large and well-known, like the *Alexandrian, Gardnerian, Druidic, Welsh Traditionalist, Georgian, Dianic* and *Church of Wicca*. Others are as small as a single coven of 13, or even a family tradition.

My wife and I established covens all over the Midwest; Dubuque and Davenport, Iowa; Madison and Milwaukee, Wisconsin; and Chicago. Over the years, we advanced to higher levels of witchcraft. Up to our departure from the city of Milwaukee in 1984, we were presiding over one of the oldest and largest networks of covens in the Midwest.

About a year after becoming a High Priest (1974), I was told by our initiators that Wicca was not what it seemed. Although much of the extant literature written by witches (and Dr. Margaret Murray's work[2]) would lead one to believe that Wicca is a survival of the ancient pagan fertility cults, especially of Northern Europe and the British Isles; there is not a shred of real historical proof for any connection between Bronze Age cults and modern witchcraft.

I learned from our initiators that it seemed that Wicca is, in fact, a manufactured religion not much older than this century. There did not seem to be evidence for any Book of Shadows (a combined "bible" and ritual book for Wiccans) much older than the 1910's!

You see, Wicca is one of Satan's "nicer" creations, tailor-made for the last half of this century. Although it may have existed for perhaps a century at most, it "came out of the broom closet" in 1951, when the British laws against witchcraft were repealed.[3] It is nothing really new, but its packaging is subtly different, tailored to a world strangling on its own technology and dying for romance, idealism and meaning.

A Cult of Deception

You may say: *"So you got sucked in too deep. So what? I've been a witch for years and never got into that satanic junk. It's just a Christian myth for real losers. As long as I stay where I am, I'm cool. I'm happy!"* That may be so, but do you honestly want to belong to a cult that deals in deception?

Let's look at the word, "Wicca," as an example. The OXFORD ENGLISH DICTIONARY reveals that the word does not mean "wise one." It means twisted, bent, or warped. Even Margot Adler admits that the word has its roots in the Indo-European roots *"wic"* or *"weik"* meaning *"to bend or to turn."* Of course, she tries to put the best possible face on it by saying that:

> "According to this view, a Witch would be a woman (or man) skilled in the art of shaping, bending and changing reality."[4]

Elsewhere, she asserts that:

> "The lexicographical (dictionary) definitions of witch are rather confusing and bear little relation to the definitions given by Witches themselves."[5]

But this is playing games, the same sort of word games most cultists play to conceal the truth. By this standard, anyone, including Anton LaVey, could say they were a witch and be right.

Yet you should hear the howls of rage among the Neo-Pagan community when even Gavin and Yvonne Frost first claimed to be witches. They couldn't be witches, they were monotheists, fakes and gay-bashers! So all of a sudden there WAS an objective standard of what makes one a witch. Yet like many things in occultism, it vanishes like mist when you try and pin it down.

In my own personal development as a witch, and the development of almost all our colleagues, I found that after about five or six years it was necessary to begin pursuing the study of the "Higher Wisdom" of Satan in order to keep growing. Magick is like a drug. You keep needing more in order to stay at a level at which you feel fulfilled. There is no end to it!

If you've stayed a Wiccan or "white" witch for a long time, it's only because you don't have enough of the Promethean itch to grow. OR it may be that you have many Christian friends or loved ones praying for you. *Did you ever think of that?*

1

Welcome To Wicca

How It Began

A fellow named Gerald B. Gardner (1884-1964) wrote a novel called HIGH MAGIC'S AID in 1949 under the pen name of Scire (his witchcraft name, from the Latin, meaning "to know"). This novel set the tone for what has become the MYTH of Wicca.

Gardner claimed there were covens of witches in Britain practicing not an anti-Christian religion, but a "Pre-Christian" religion. This, he claimed, was called Wicca. In his later writings he finally revealed that he belonged to a rare, surviving coven in the New Forest vicinity of England which could trace its form of worship back thousands of years to Paleolithic times.

This, he asserted, was the "Old Religion," an animistic worship of the principles of nature and reproduction; rather like a warmed-over rehash of Fraser's anthropological chestnut, THE GOLDEN BOUGH. The gods of this Old Religion were a supreme Mother Goddess who ruled the earth, the moon, the sea, and things agricultural. Her secret name (in his coven anyway) was ARAYDA. There was also a

Horned God who ruled the sun and hunting, who was variously called Herne, Cernunnos or Pan.

Thus, Wicca was not an attack on Christianity, but was supposedly a much older religion whose gods were old when Yahweh of the Bible was in knee pants. According to Gardner, witches worshipped naked (or "skyclad" as he preferred to call it) and were matriarchal; since the goddess is eternal, while the god grows old, dies, and is reborn every year.

**Portrait of
Gerald Gardner,
father of modern Wicca**

Gardner's "Wiccans" danced naked in a ring within a magick[1] circle, had ritual sex on solemn occasions, and whipped one another ceremonially to purify and raise the power.

"Revisionist" historians in contemporary Wicca, such as Francis King and Elliot Rose,[2] have suggested that Gardner may have set up his cult in this way because he came from a family of devout nudists and had become addicted to what is discreetly called masochism (sexual stimulation from being whipped by a domineering woman.) If so, it may be the first time in modern history that a religion was founded just to indulge someone's perversities.

The "Old Religion" Gets Going!

From Gardner, an entire cult grew. Being no man's fool, he got involved in Cecil H. Williamson's "Museum of Magic and Witchcraft" in Castledown on the Isle of Man off the British coast and tried to turn it into a witchy Disneyland of sorts, but died before achieving his goal.[3]

Amid howls of sacrilege from Wiccans the world over, this museum was recently sold by Gardner's magical heiress, Monique Wilson, to RIPLEY'S BELIEVE IT OR NOT and moved, lock, stock and broomstick, to America.[4] Before the museum arrived in the U.S., it was preceded by "Gardnerian Wicca," which was carried to these shores in the 1960's primarily by Raymond Buckland and his High Priestess wife, Rosemary (since divorced).

The weed of Wicca mutated as it spread and

many offshoots developed. The largest and best known of these was the group to which we belonged, *Alexandrian Wicca*. This was founded by Alex Sanders, self-styled **"King of the Witches,"** who claimed that his brand of Wicca was much older and truer than Gardner's because he was directly descended from the 15th century King of the Witches, Owen Glendowner through his grandmother.

Sanders' brand of Wicca claimed to have access to higher degrees than Gardner's, and emphasized in addition to the traditional circle ceremonies and sabbats, elements of ceremonial magick and qabalism much more than did Gardner. Otherwise, the rites were similar. Alex Sanders was also a showman. He took his covens to nightclubs where they were billed as "Alex Sanders and His Topless Witches." Probably no male witch was photographed more than Sanders, with his young, lovely, blonde wife Maxine (who divorced him in the late 1970's). Although recently deceased, Sanders' pictures can still be seen in such books as MAN, MYTH AND MAGIC.

By the early '70's, there were dozens of traditions of Wicca; some splintered off Gardner or Sanders but most were totally original. There were ethnic witches like the Welsh Traditionalists (headed by a homosexual, Ed Bucyzinksi), Georgian, Nordic, Sicilian Stregoi, Hispanic Brujeria and the Druidic Craft from Scotland, plus the controversial but highly successful *Church of Wicca* of Gavin and Yvonne Frost.

The Neo-Pagans

Then there were groups which made no effort to pretend they were anything but artificial religions, made up out of whole cloth, but emulating many of the doctrines of Wicca. These would include Tim and Julie Zell's *Church of All Worlds* (also long divorced and remarried), Frederick Adams' *Feraferia* and Harold Moss' *Church of the Eternal Source.*

There are many differences between these dozens of groups. Some worked nude, others robed. Some whipped, most didn't. Some used ritual sex or even orgies, some abstained. A few common elements can be found, though, in all Wicca and Neo-Paganism:

1) A polytheistic world-view; usually a god/goddess pair.
2) A belief in "westernized" reincarnation (no moving backward to incarnate as animals, just moving forward to be reborn as humans).
3) A shamanic worldview similar to animism (the belief that all objects have life and souls) which includes strong ecological overtones and often an openness to some drugs.
4) Most are militantly feminist and politically left-wing, even anarchistic; although there are exceptions.
5) A "do your own thing" morality, as long as it doesn't "hurt anybody." This often included free sexual activity at least

within the group.

6) An "Aquarian" view of human destiny — the seed bed from which was grown much of the New Age movement — the notion that persons can evolve spiritually through their own efforts and ultimately attain either enlightenment or even godhood.

It is easy to see that with values like this, Wicca took off like a rocket among the "hippie" generation of which we were members.

It appealed to the Rousseauistic idea of "Humankind as noble savages," dancing free and naked in the woods; worshipping the forces of nature, living in harmony with that nature and above all, bucking the "establishment." Native Americans were surprised to find themselves considered (sometimes to their dismay) homegrown, ethnic witches or pagans.

Wicca and Neo-paganism were thus an intriguing blend of a dislike of technology and a romanticization of ancient cultures combined with a passionate interest in fantasy and science fiction.

To this intriguing philosophical stew, Satan added such notions as ecology, environmental awareness and feminism. Although formulated in the early part of this century, Wicca was actually tailor-made for the counter-culture in the sixties. Clearly Satan plans his work well in advance.

An "Old Religion For A New Age"

Satan knew that classical or "Gothic" satanism (as we called it) would lose much of its bite after the sixties. In a time of topless beaches and "free" sex, who would be titillated by a nude woman on an altar? The High liturgies of Catholicism were waning, so who would be aroused by rites which blasphemed ceremonies to which serious attention was no longer paid? In an age when "respectable theologians" denied the divinity or resurrection of Christ and God was pronounced dead, what was left to shock?

You see, we contended that Satanism was just a perversion, a liturgical heresy, if you will, of Christianity.[5] We claimed that Wicca, on the other hand, was an older, purer faith which stood on its own merits.

There is no denying that the Christian body was in need of revival! By engineering Wicca, Satan was able to do an end-run around established churches and create a religion which seemed vital, exciting, anarchistic, contemporary and relevant; yet would also appear ancient and timeless. As Neo-pagan writer Tim (now "Otter") Zell put it, it would be an "old religion for a new age."

Wicca was able to provide an ideology that would tickle the ears of the idealistic young people, while at the same time throw the materialistic hypocrisy of their culture into stark relief. Satan loves spiritual vacuums, because he rushes in with a deceptive religious "toy" to fill that vacuum!

Thus, the Devil tried to dance in and co-opt an entire generation. In my education, by the time I was old enough to begin to chose my life path, my church had deserted its spiritual foundation and became thoroughly enamored of social action and psychiatry.

To find the spiritual vitality I so desperately craved, I needed to look elsewhere; and liberal professors and writers from my own denomination were there with their bookshelves full of neo-gnosticism, psychiatry and situational ethics.

There is nothing Satan (or his followers) love more than to take a young, relatively innocent idealist and corrupt him, and my story may be all too typical.

Things Aren't What They Seem Here

As mentioned earlier, we stepped deeply into the Craft and learned that things were not as they seemed. In spite of this somewhat disillusioning news, I was determined to continue in the Craft. Both my High Priestess (whom I shortly thereafter married) and I decided to establish our own covens and train witches in the priesthood of the Great Mother — the supreme deity of Wiccans. My wife and I moved to Milwaukee, a much larger city, in response to requests from more than 40 would-be witches that we set up classes and covens for them.

We studied hard and practiced what we preached, living our religion. As a result, we were highly esteemed by both our students and our colleagues; and the number of our initiates grew rapidly.

It was only after years of ritual work and research that the truth finally began to be unveiled. Behind the benign face of the goddess of witchcraft lurked a much darker, dangerous side. I had learned from our teacher that the Book of Shadows (our witches' "bible" or rule and law book) was probably the result of a collaboration between Gerald Gardner and the notorious satanist, Aleister Crowley.[6] New witches were usually led to believe the Book of Shadows was centuries old.

The issue of the degree to which Crowley was involved in the creation of Gardnerian ritual is highly controversial. Two leading chroniclers of contemporary Wicca, Doreen Valiente and Margot Adler, both admit connections are there and that there is a lot of nonsense circulated about supposedly "ancient" witch rituals. In fact, Valiente admits that a chant, "The Witch's Rune," which we were taught was centuries old, actually was written by her and Gerald Gardner in the 1950's![7]

The aforementioned occult historian Francis King, wrote that Gardner hired Crowley...

> "...at a generous fee, to write elaborate rituals for the new 'Gardnerian' witch-

cult and, at about the same time, either forged or procured to be forged, the so-called Book of Shadows, allegedly a sixteenth century witches' rule book, but betraying its modern origins in every line of its unsatisfactory pastiche of Elizabethan English."[8]

Other writers deny that Crowley's influence on the book was that great. Adler, a Wiccan herself, claims that "there has never been a single piece of real proof that Crowley was hired to write the Gardnerian rituals.[9] Methinks the lady doth protest too much. Sizeable chunks of the Great Rite ceremony are right out of the Crowleyan "bible," LIBER AL VEL LEGIS[10] and his Gnostic Mass, both published years before the Gardner material saw daylight.

Doreen Valiente herself, who was an intimate associate of Gardner's during his last fifteen years, is quoted in Adler's book as saying that the Book of Shadows rituals were:

> "...heavily influenced by Crowley and the O.T.O. (Crowley's Masonic/sex magic society), but underneath, there was a lot which wasn't Crowley at all, and wasn't the Golden Dawn (another Rosicrucian/ Masonic society) or ceremonial magic either...(she was) responsible for quite a lot of the *wording* of the present-day rituals; *but not the framework of those rituals or the ideas upon which they are based.*" (italics author's)[11]

Thus, we began to see where time honored truths and "ancient mysteries" were actually falsehoods, benign falsehoods perhaps, but dishonesty, nonetheless. In the mid '70's, the "Myth of Wicca" had already begun to crumble, both from attacks from cowans (non-witches) and from serious witches like our initiators who had dared to open their eyes, investigate their origins and admit that the "emperor" had no clothes (in more ways than one).

However, we learned that all this was okay, because "myths" could be true, even if they were false.

Carl Jung's Influence

These facts didn't bother us much, because like most Wiccans of the time, we were utilitarians. We felt that if it worked, it didn't matter if it was true or not. In this, we were influenced by the work of occult-psychologist Carl G. Jung, who taught that myths had a life of their own and that even if they weren't literally true, if enough people believed in them, they were invested with a mighty, archetypal power all their own.

Many of today's young Wiccans accept this, and Jung is one of the patron "saints" of the Neo-Pagan/New Age movement. In fact, the "educated opinion" among most witches now is that there isn't exactly a real god or goddess, but that they are simply archetypes — images in the minds of the devotees.[12]

Jung felt that there were archetypal images or formularies which existed deep in the subterranean unconsciousness of people.[13] This region he called the "Collective Unconscious." It was from this region that all dream images came, and all of the images with which people invest their religious faith.

Thus, it didn't matter if Gardner's story was true in real, 20th century Europe; because he may have been tapping into ancient memories and myths to which he had little tangible connection. He was supposedly drinking from the taproot of the collective unconscious and bringing forth deeper meaning concerning the Goddess (or Anima principle in Jung's terms) for our time. Thus, Gardner's religion could be a myth and still be "true," at least in psychoanalytic terms.

It is now a matter of common knowledge that much of Gardner's story is fiction. Yet, most witches aren't bothered by that. Since the seventies, many witches wanted to be totally creative and make up their religion out of their heads — without trying to make any pretentious claims about having "unbroken lines of power" back to medieval "Kings" of the witches. Most Neo-pagan groups fall into this category. They are based on myths, fantasy or even science-fiction stories. Therefore, these "revisionist" views of Wicca's background meant little to us.

Other things began to close in on me, though. Although I had primarily joined Wicca as a religion, like most members, I was intrigued by the idea of psychic powers and the ability to do miraculous things. As a beginning witch, the magick worked spectacularly! I did spells, and could truly affect people with things like healings or prosperity.

But now, as a High Priest, even with increased dedication to the ideals of the goddess, I began finding that the magick was losing its zing. Our students were still able to have success with their spells, but ours seemed to be falling flat. It was finally pointed out to me that to rectify this, it would be necessary to pursue the "left-hand path."

Both in my studies and in my "trance work" with my familiar spirits and spirit guides, it became increasingly apparent that there was not a clear boundary between so-called white and black witchcraft. I know, because I slid across it fairly easily. Witches have no firm sense of ethics. We started out like many Wiccans, refusing to do any kind of magick which would influence people against their will.

We sincerely believed in and followed the Wiccan Rede,[14] which taught that *"an it harm none, do what ye will,"* which was perilously close to Aleister Crowley's commandment *"Do what thou wilt shall be the whole of the law."* Then coveners started coming to us saying that their loved ones needed healing, so we wrestled with healing people without their knowledge. Was that alright?

Moral Dilemmas

Coveners came to the circles with problems in their families and sought help from the group. Could we help these people? As High Priestess and High Priest, we thought we knew what was "best" for these loved ones. Should they be married? Then put a love spell on them. Should they have a better job? Then do a prosperity spell on them. We slid along the continuum and used increasing levels of witchcraft power for supposedly altruistic reasons.

Then a covener comes and says that his wife, supposedly a vile individual, has divorced him and has custody of the children. He says that it is in the best interest of the kids to be kept away from her. Could we put a spell on her to kill her for the sake of him and the little ones? You see, when you are in leadership positions and you have hurting, needful people coming to you with questions like that, it starts getting harder and harder to make those kind of absolute choices on the basis of a bland axiom like "The Wiccan Rede:" *"An it harm none, do what ye will."*

Is it "the greater good for the greater number?" Do the lives of two or three innocent children outweigh the life of one hateful mother? Or is life an absolute? You can imagine how things get a little blurry despite your best intentions.

Into The Underworld

Then we discovered that our teachers, people we

had come to thoroughly respect and regard as ideal role models, felt that in order for us to grow and become more "evolved," we needed to come into a relationship with the Lord of the Underworld. The Second Grade[15] of our rite of Wicca contained the ritual drama, *"The Descent of the Goddess into the Underworld."*

Here the Goddess, the ultimate deity of Wicca, descends to the lower depths of the earth to determine why the living things of her natural kingdom must age and die. She is stripped of all her clothing and jewels, bound and brought before the Dark Lord of Death, the darker aspect of Cernunnos or Lucifer, the Horned God of Wicca.

He falls in love with her and proposes to her. In turn, she rebukes him because he causes all the things she loves to wither and die. He tells her if she will not be his bride, she must kneel to his scourge. As she kneels, bound and nude, in fetal position, he whips her. She then cries, (oddly enough) "I know the pangs of love."

Ultimately, as the rite says, "they loved and were one." The Lord of Death gives her a necklace which symbolizes the circle of rebirth or reincarnation, the Wiccan's hope of immortality; and teaches her its mysteries. Then a teaching is given on how the purpose of Wicca is to lead priests and priestesses into eternal marriage relationships through many lifetimes as "soulmates."[16]

This is the central drama of classic Wicca,

occupying a place analogous to the death and resurrection of Jesus in Christianity, and is based on an ancient Sumerian legend of "The Descent of Innanna." Why do I mention it?

Because this drama is the key to the corruption which takes place in the Wiccan believer's heart, at least in those who follow classic Wicca such as we did. I'm certain Satan has other methods he uses on those who do not follow the Gardnerian/Alexandrian Book of Shadows.

Confronting The Shadow

I was told that rite had deeper meanings, which I was beginning to realize. Just as the Goddess, who represents all that is good and idealistic in Wicca, had to descend to the depths of the underworld to truly be fulfilled in her love; so we had to plumb the depths of our own psyches and confront the dark sides of our own nature, in Jungian terms, the "Shadow."

The Shadow is the dark side of our nature — all the evil and perverse fantasies and ego drives that polite society will not tolerate. Therefore these drives are submerged into the bottom of the psyche where they tend to fester and erupt in nightmares or even, in worst case scenarios, violent psychotic breakdowns. Jung felt that many of the problems of the world came because people totally ignored their Shadow and repressed it. He advocated that they deal with the Shadow and acknowledge it through fantasy, therapy or role playing.

Magic took this concept and brought it home with incredible power through the force of symbolic magical rituals and shamanic acts.

I had to absorb my Shadow, my personal darkness, the darkest part of my nature which I never exposed to anyone. I had to "love it and become one with it" even as the Great Mother had to love and mate with the Dark Lord. Thus, the two opposites: life and death, beauty and ugliness, love and hate, good and evil, could fuse and become one in my personal life.

Just as the Great Mother had to be stripped and tied and rendered vulnerable before the Dark Lord, so my psyche would have to lay aside its notions and defenses and stand before the Shadow naked and without pre-conceptions. This is how I was taught to deal with sin, although the word was never used, of course.

This, I was told, was a key part of the "shamanic task."[17] I would have to open my psyche to all my personal "demons" and allow them to meld together with all that was good within me. Thus, I could become an Adept and attain *"The Knowledge and Conversation of The Holy Guardian Angel"* In qabalistic terms, this meant meeting my higher self or "god-self," the part of me which was eternally god-conscious or divine.

As I began my shamanic task, I descended into the underworld both ritually and psycho-logically. This is the step which destroys! Wicca itself is bad enough, in a Biblical context; but this process is where the masks come off and things are seen as they are!

But what would you do in that dilemma? What would you do if you followed the advice of these teachers and authors and then, after a few more years, discovered that this "Shadow" to which you had been yielding was Satan?

Today, for example, the situation has become even more blatant. Things which were not readily committed to print in the sixties and seventies have now become well-known through the writings of leading thinkers in the Wicca movement. The chief theologian and educator of Wicca in this country seems to be Miriam Starhawk, a woman who was just beginning to make her presence known nationally when we were involved in Wicca. She has written:

> "The depths of our beings are not all sunlit; to see clearly we must be able to dive into the dark, inner abyss and *Acknowledge the creatures we may find there.*"[18]

This is precisely the lesson given by the Legend of the Goddess' descent, and it is by following the advice of such eminent Wiccan leaders as Ms. Starhawk that we began to realize that the mask had fallen off our "Horned Lord" and revealed him as Satan!

Nor is Starhawk a lone crackpot voice. Others,

echoing her Jungian psychological rationale even more explicitly, have recently counseled:

> "The shadow...the beast, the devil...is the multifarious figure whose features can be detected somewhere behind the persona-mask of every man and woman. It is the beast that haunts every beauty, the monster that awaits the hero on his quest. But if we recognize, acknowledge and come to terms with it, a great deal of knowledge formerly hidden, unconscious, in the shadows, becomes conscious. When we recognize this devil as an aspect of ourselves, then the **SHADOW** functions as a teacher and initiator ... providing us with the greatest gift of all, self-understanding."[19]

Prominent Neo-Pagan teacher and Dominican Catholic priest, Matthew Fox, who advises the church of Jesus to return to practicing "white" witchcraft, has also said:

> "God is 'superessential darkness' and to make contact with the darkness is to make contact with the deepest side of the Godhead."[20]

Fox also advises that the:

> "very act of entering darkness, to befriend it, becomes a profoundly healing event."[21]

Texe Marrs, in his excellent book, MYSTERY

MARK OF THE NEW AGE, cites many New Age/Wiccan (the two are really just different sides of the same spiritual coin) thinkers who teach the same thing our teachers and "spirit guides" taught us in the 1970's. He quotes Rainer Maria Wilkie as saying that we must love and accept the "dragons" within us and that we must go ever deeper into the darkness to discover the roots of our existence.[22]

He also quotes Jack Underhill, editor of the Life Times magazine as saying we "understand Good better when we have met *intimately*, with what is called evil." (emphasis added)[23]

I trust this establishes that the "expose yourself to the darkness" teaching is not something unique to my own mind, but rather something which is woven into the very warp and woof of all non-Christian mysticism, New Age thought and Wicca. Some pretty heavy thinkers were talking about it even back in the 1970's.

Turning Up The Heat

What would you do if you were told that "evolved people" realized that in order to truly reconcile the yin and yang within you, the positive-negative polarities, in order to become "individuated" (the ultimate goal of your psyche in Jung's writings) you have to surrender to Satan? What would you think if some people you respected the most told you to yield yourself to the darkest parts of your own psyche? Think about it!

I didn't just become a "luciferian" overnight. Little by little the masks slip off as you are made ready by your "spirit guides" for greater and greater Light. It's the old story of the frog in the pan of water. You turn up the heat gradually enough, and he doesn't even know he is being boiled. In Wicca, Satan turns up the heat gradually enough that you do not know you are being delicately enfolded in his embrace — until it is too late.

At first my quest was for "Individuation," (union with my Shadow and becoming an Adept.)[24] At that point, I knew one of the pre-eminent names of the god of the witches was Lucifer.[25] Then I learned that the Horned God, Lucifer, had a "Shadow" as well. I'll bet you didn't know God had a sinful side, did you? He does for Jung, and for most Pagans. In fact, I was taught that Jesus himself had to go through this same experience in order to become individuated and in contact with his feminine side.[26]

Just as the sun is bright at noonday but disappears into the bowels of the earth at night (apparently); so does the light of Lucifer become the brilliant darkness of Satan — yet it is the same god!

All these paradoxes may be found in the Legend of the Goddess; and in the way modern Wiccans interpreted it according to Jung's occult belief. In a gradual, almost effortless segue, the "White Witch" becomes a Luciferian, and finally a satanist!

Many Wiccans have said that I fell into temptations of selfishness and power-tripping — that I left the "true" Wicca for the "Christian heresy" of satanism for reasons of power. First of all, I ask what in the name of common sense is "true Wicca?" If the whole background of Gardner, et.al. was stitched together out of fragments of history, myth and fiction, then it cannot be the "true Wicca."

That leaves the current theological concept, as elucidated in books like Adler's **DRAWING DOWN THE MOON,** that Wicca is basically a created, "creative" religion, drawing on ancient archetypes to heal the self and the land. Even then, there are literally dozens of kinds of Wicca, as we have seen. If *we* followed our personal "myths" and archetypes, *how can the faith we arrived at not be true?* Who is to say it is false Wicca? The bottom line, my friends, is that in Wicca, truth is what you make it.

Concerning our supposed lust for power, as may be seen from the above account, power was barely even a consideration. Power was a convenient fringe-benefit, nothing more. I became a satanist because:

a) People I loved, respected and trusted told me that I should;

b) Writers within and without the pagan scene, like Jung, Nietzsche, Spangler and others, led one to believe that true wholeness could only be comprehended by totally assimilating the universe in all its aspects.

35

The Lie of Monism

This is the key concoction of monism, and most Wiccans and New Agers are monists! Monists believe that all is One. The God/Goddess is all — and all is God/Goddess — and everything is a part of It.[27] This philosophy makes an easy slide into satanism an all-too-real possibility!

But if all is a part of God/Goddess, then ***nothing can be evil.*** If nothing can be evil, then even Satan becomes an archetype to be reconciled within your own psyche (to use Jungian terms). Even if Satan is only a Christian head-trip, he still is an archetype to be reckoned with; he is a reservoir of vast power because of the strange people down through the years who have believed in him. You cannot move in the realms of the psyche without confronting him.

I never sought power from satanism — at first. I never sought to exploit people with satanism — at first. If confidentiality permitted it, I could give you the names of dozens of people who personally studied under us, and I don't think one of them would accuse me of being on a power trip or exploitative until the very end.

I tried to treat everyone in our groups with a true servant heart. We frequently opened our home to our poorer friends because we felt Craft law demanded it. We never cursed anyone until the final years when the power of Satan started really taking hold. I never even tried to use my position to get into bed with the women in our groups! I regarded all as goddesses in the making and treated them with utmost respect.

Wisdom — Not Power!

What I sought from satanism was knowledge — wisdom, "undefiled wisdom," to use Anton LaVey's term![28] I earnestly craved that wisdom, which I thought would be essential for our well-being and development as whole human beings. I wanted to be wise! Isn't that the goal of any witch? The problem is that sooner or later you discover that the "wisdom" you possess holds you like a fly in amber and all the superb intentions in the world do not keep you from being dragged down into a morass of evil!

The last few years I did what I now consider to be horrid things. I exploited people to a greater extent, but that was primarily because the forces I was trying to manipulate had such an iron grip on me that my conscience strangled.

I came to the point where my sense of ethics had been totally swallowed up in expediency and elitist lies. I felt that people who opposed our goals should be slain with curses for their own karmic well-being, because next lifetime they would "know better." Women would now be drawn into my bed because it would "help their spiritual evolution" to have sex with a being as evolved as I.

It was taken for granted that the occasional animals needed for sacrifice would be slain without mercy knowing that, in reward, they would come back as human beings in their next lifetime.[29] People who willingly gave their lives for Lucifer would come back as gods or goddesses! I was perfectly prepared to let myself be ritually slain if necessary, for the greater glory of the gods!

You see, anything can eventually melt into the morass of monism! Without a solid rock to depend on like Jesus Christ, you are totally awash; and the heart is desperately wicked and deceitful in getting what it wants (Jeremiah 17:9). Believe me, all the idealistic intentions in the world won't help once you've taken one step too many onto the path of paganism.

The Path Downward

I learned that Lucifer was the true power behind Wicca, and that as a High Priest, I would have to do his bidding if I wanted to continue to evolve. Again, note that at first the name "Lucifer" was used. Wiccans are first taught that Satan is a Biblical myth, and a slander on the true god of light, Lucifer. We liked to quote Dr. Margaret Murray and say, "The gods of the old religion become the devils of the new."

We felt that Lucifer and the Great Mother, Diana, had been venerated for millennia until the Biblical bully, Jehovah, moved in and insisted that His was the only game in town. I remember one highly respected Wiccan leader saying that the God of the Bible was a "male-chauvinist piggy with the manners of a 5-year-old brat."

I am ashamed to say this, but the sweet, "white-light" Neo-Pagan organization, THE CHURCH OF ALL WORLDS, to which we belonged, was founded by a fellow named Tim Zell, who once gave a talk entitled **"The Great Mother versus The Great Mother-F———."** Such was the level of regard for Judeo-Christianity. But we weren't satanists — oh <u>no</u>!

We felt that with the institutionalization of Christianity in the fourth century, all the true secrets of Jesus had been destroyed and that the true, older religion of Wicca had been driven underground.[30] Its goddess, Diana or Arayda, became the Blessed Virgin Mary. Cathedrals were built on the old pagan sacred groves; but there was no room in Catholicism for another god, so the Horned God, Lucifer or Cernunnos, got demoted to playing "devil."

The witches with whom I was acquainted even believed that Jesus Himself was a witch, with his "coven" of Himself and 12 apostles. They believed that the institutional church had censored the Bible to remove all references to reincarnation and Jesus' occultism and "witchiness," but we insiders knew the truth.

So we believed that Lucifer (often known as Bel, Lugh, Herne, Faunus, Pan or Cernunnos) was the true God and that Satan was a boogy-man manufactured by the Christians. Of course, that was just what Satan wanted us to believe.

The Crowley Connection

So I began studying the darker side of magick.
Aleister Crowley was of course a part of the
serious study of any kind of ceremonial magick,
although some magicians tried to pretend he
wasn't there. We got seriously into Crowley,
who was certainly the wittiest, classiest and
most honest writer on magick in this century.

Two photographs of Aleister Crowley

A comment needs to be made about Crowley's
involvement with Wicca. Two of the leading
public figures in modern Wicca have definite
links with Crowley (who died in '47), *about
which they boast.* A third, Gardner, has been
linked with Crowley in the writing of the Book
of Shadows. Sybil Leek, now deceased, was one
of the best known "white" witches on either side

40

of the Atlantic. Her book, DIARY OF A WITCH, was my first contact with the concept of Wicca.

As a young woman, Leek supposedly knew and admired Crowley, who boasted of being "the wickedest man in the world." He openly despised Christ and the faith of his parents (who happened to be Plymouth Brethren). She studied under him and asserts that he had a profound influence on her life. Leek also boasted that Crowley's mantle was passed onto her.[31]

There are definite evidences in history that Gardner may have commissioned Crowley to write parts of the *Book of Shadows*.[32] They seem to have been acquaintances, if not friends. If Crowley was such an evil satanist (and he was), why should the "godfather" of modern Wicca have been associated with him; **unless Wicca was simply clever packaging for satanism?**

Alex Sanders, mentioned earlier as the initiator of our initiators and certainly one of the most influential Wiccans of the last 25 years, claimed to have known Crowley and studied under him.[33] He also wears a magic ring identical to one which Crowley used to wear and casually let it be known among his friends that Crowley had bestowed it upon him. Sanders has even been quoted in a book that if a certain writer did not behave himself, Sanders would "...do things to him that would make Aleister Crowley look like a (censored) boy scout."[34]

That last remark could have been meant in jest,

but it illustrates my point. If Wiccans aren't satanists, why do two of its prominent spokespeople take such pains to associate themselves with the century's leading satanist?

Why do so-called "white" witches continually write such complimentary things about a man like Crowley?[35] Why does a respected Wiccan/ Neo-pagan scholar like Margot Adler write that "ecumenical gatherings" of Neo-pagan groups almost always affirm Crowley's cardinal ethical teachings[36] (a man whose "ethics" consisted of driving women to drink and his men to commit suicide; racism, sexism and anti-semitism)?? Why is the "Wiccan Rede" so close to his BOOK OF THE LAW?

Why are virtually all of his major books included in Wiccan bibliographies?[37] It would be like a Christian claiming to have inherited the mantle of Judas Iscariot or recommending the writings of Attila the Hun!

Unless, of course, there is more than meets the eye here; and there are things the "big folks" know that the little "witches in the pew" don't know about Wicca. Both Leek and Sanders bend over backwards to assure us that Wiccans don't believe in Satan-worship. Then they cuddle up to "The Great Beast" himself. It is a paradox which bears thought.

Things Get Darker

In any event, I revered Alex Sanders. The fact

that he seemed to be recommending Crowley made it that much easier for me to read his books. Like many Wiccans, I began with Crowley by thinking, *"I'll just take the helpful thoughts and leave the diabolical things alone."*

I learned that I was whistling in the dark. One might as readily say, *"I'll drive my car, but leave the gasoline alone."* Perhaps a year went by and I was given Anton Szandor LaVey's book, THE SATANIC BIBLE. Again, the implication at first was that LaVey was a little perverse, but there were helpful things in the book that every High Priest should know.

Indeed there were!

As I studied, I realized that although Wiccans generally avoid the inverted pentagram of satanism, the symbol of Second Degree which was traced on my body in oil, wine and kisses as I was made a Wiccan High Priest <u>was indeed the inverted pentagram.</u> I wondered how could it be evil if it was the sign of Second Degree?

The more I learned, the more I realized that sooner or later I was going to need answers. On one hand, I was told that satanists were demented Christians, but on the other, I kept discovering satanic symbols, names and philosophies in "white" witchcraft.

Finally, I was told condescendingly by my teachers that the concept of Wicca was something for neophytes to believe; but as a

43

potential adept, I would have to plumb the depths of the goddess' descent into the underworld.

It all began to make sense, in a dangerous and thrilling way. With dwindling reluctance, I began to seriously research LaVey. As I practiced his formulas of magick, my sense of worth and well-being began to swell. Although we did not tell those students under us, I joined the Church of Satan and began receiving their materials. My seduction was nearly complete.

As I advanced in ceremonial magick, which is taught after Third Degree, I got profoundly into Crowley. It became apparent to me that he had been a real trail-blazer in 20th century occultism. Trying to practice serious magick and ignoring Crowley's contribution would be like trying to ignore an elephant in your bedroom.

A Revelation of Satan!

I progressed in LaVey's order and was finally made a Warlock in the Church of Satan, which was the satanic Second Degree.[38] As a reward for this achievement, Satan played his trump card. I was doing studies in Crowley's Book of the Law and the Book of Revelation in the Bible for my quabalistic research when I read the famous passage in Rev.13:18 about the number of the Beast. I had a blinding, soul-searing "revelation" of my own!

I was overwhelmed with a pillar of astral light.

Although I saw no person and heard no audible voice, I KNEW with an unshakable certainty that Rev.13:18 was the answer I had sought. *Contained within its numerology was the secret that Aleister Crowley was a reincarnation of Jesus Christ!*

I was driven to my knees by the sublime beauty of this truth; and felt the power of magick upon me as never before. I felt as if I was floating. Nothing like this had ever happened to me before, and I took it as a message from the gods. This was followed by other "miracles" which served to confirm my insight, including wine turning into genuine human blood at a Catholic mass I celebrated.

Quite soon after that, I was brought in touch with higher ranking satanists from Chicago. I was initiated into their circle by signing a covenant with Satan for my soul. (I didn't know it already belonged to him.)

Though the rites now began to include blood sacrifice (including my own) I was not deterred. When I first became a witch, my perineum was cut and my blood was shed. I knew this was a pallid echo of the ancient sacrifice of castration expected of the priests of the Great Mother in Greece and I was honored to receive it.[39]

I knew Crowley had used blood in his rites and even the classic Wiccans used the scourge occasionally on rare ceremonies when blood needed to be shed![40] Hadn't even Jesus been sacrificed in a blood rite for his own Father?

This knowledge or illumination I'd received —
that Jesus and Crowley were the same spirit in
different incarnations — put the imprimatur
upon just about everything the satanic crowd
did. I soon learned that LaVey's church was just
the tip of the iceberg. His kind of satanism,
though certainly the most visible, was too
"goody-goody" for my crowd. They regarded him
as a money-making showman.

Sanitized Satanism?

I'd realized that Wicca, the religion our disciples
were following was just a slightly sanitized
version of continental Satan-worship! We still
taught them that it was just a charming little
nature cult with herbs and circles and whips,
but we knew better. We knew real wisdom came
from Satan! It now became clear to me that
witchcraft was rather like an onion or an
artichoke. You had layers upon layers of
meaning and secrets!

We knew this in a limited way, even as
beginners. We were told that the way to set up
a coven was to start public lectures on an
apparently innocent subject such as astrology or
parapsychology. From the responses to that
lecture, we would find people who truly wanted
to learn more.

These people would become students in classes
with our Spiritualist church, or with the *Mental*

Science Institute, the legal front for the Druidic witches. They would study psychic development or ESP or astrology. Then those who wanted to learn more would be told that the basis of all these things was an ancient, innocent nature religion called Wicca. It was to these people, and these people only, that the word "WITCH" was ever mentioned.

These people were further screened and enrolled in classes for initiation into Wicca, then we would start the cycle over with a whole new bunch.

Although I thought that as a Third Grade Witch High Priest, I was on the inside of the artichoke, I now discovered that I was only in the *middle* layer. Wiccans like myself, who were hungry for more wisdom, would learn about Lucifer. Luciferians who needed more were eventually drawn into the Anton LaVey level of satanism, still relatively innocuous.[41] Then the Church of Satan members who were really "evolved" would actually be led into hard-core satanism.

This is the stage I was now at, and I could only look back and smile at how naive I was. I thought that witchcraft was just gathering herbs and dancing naked in the forest, but now I realized it was the threshold of the dark, passionate thrills of the kingdom of Satan, or the "Kingdom," as we called it.

The man who was my immediate superior was a strange, but powerful satanist from Chicago with all sorts of connections in politics and industry. I was amazed at the people of power I would meet at the sabbats.

I figured I had it made and my ship was finally coming in. I signed a pact in my own blood with Satan. He received complete control of my body and soul. In return, I got seven years of whatever I desired: money, sex, drugs or power! It could all be mine!

But I didn't realize that there was a flaw in my plans.

The Power of Prayer

I'd sent in a check to the Church of Satan. When it came back from the bank, a note was written on it in a delicate, feminine hand: *"I'll be praying for you in Jesus' name."* A woman at the bank had noticed to whom the check was drafted and decided to intercede for miserable me before the throne of Almighty God!

I sneered at the check. After all, I thought, Jesus had been a witch. He did what I did! He approved, because he'd reincarnated as a world-class satanist himself!

Within *days,* things began to happen. I lost my job, my wife got sick, I got sick, and my satanic mentor, so powerful and self-assured, got in a serious truck accident and ended up in the hospital with grievous abdominal injuries. His previously limitless supply of money from

California dried up, and I was effectively cut off from all my powerful new contacts.

Although I was still practicing magick and finding new innocent college students every month to sign a pact with Satan, I found that my magick power was drying up again. My psychic powers and intuition were fogging over, and nothing I could do would bring it back! I got desperate! I began doing spells and praying to my god for some kind of sign as to what we were doing wrong.

Now I praise God for this, because if things had kept going well, I never would have kept searching. I thought I had all the answers, in the "undefiled wisdom" of Satan. But the Lord God was breaking me and molding me into a more fit vessel for His service. It would take five years of searching and a perilous time in the dreadful crucible of Mormonism, that clever counterfeit of Christianity, before I would really come to know Jesus Christ as my Lord and Savior; but that, as they say, is another tale.

Suffice it to say, I learned that Wicca is a sweet, beguiling, but dangerous fantasy. I pray that in the remainder of this book, I can demonstrate how truly dangerous it is.

2

Wiccan "Public Relations"

Much of my personal story as contained in chapter one is radically different from the current public relations image being promoted in the media by witches and Neo-Pagans.

Like the PR material for any deceptive religious cult, they wish to present as positive an image as possible. They deal in non-issues rather than the central points which really matter in an eternal perspective. However, when the actual experience of thousands of Wiccans and Neo-Pagans who come to Jesus Christ runs completely contrary to what is being presented in the PR material, we have to wonder about "truth in packaging."

An Official Statement

As I was preparing this book, a flyer from the Witches' League for Public Awareness written by "official witch" Laurie Cabot came into my hands. I'm going to quote from it and comment as appropriate, so you can see how the current breed of witch is attempting to present herself.

The Witches of Salem Present
The Do's and Don't of Witchcraft

1. Witches do not do evil. They believe that doing evil and harm is against the Universal Law. Witchcraft tells us, "An it harm none, do what ye will."

2. Witches do not worship Satan. They do not have a Satan in their deity structure.

3. Witches wear clothing of every style and color. They come from every socio-economic and ethnic background...

4. A male Witch is not a warlock. This was a term used by Christians during the "Burning Time" to designate male Witches.

5. Witches do use spells. A spell is a thought, a projection, a prayer or an enchantment. Other religions use prayer, meditation, projection or ritual to produce an intended result. The word 'spell' does not equate with doing evil or harm.

6. Witches do use magic wands ... they are used for directing energy, as in healing...

7. Witches do use Witchcraft as a Science, an Art and a Religion. They use their knowledge and magic in harmony with the Universe and Nature around them. The word 'magic' comes from the Greek word 'magi' meaning 'wise. In the origins of many languages, the word 'Witch' was part of a constellation of words for 'wise' or 'wise ones.'...

8. In Witchcraft as a Science, we view the

pentacle as the golden section, a geometric shape and a talisman. In the Religion of Witchcraft, the circle surrounding the star represents God/Goddess — the total intelligence refracting and reflecting all light. Light gives us wisdom. The five pointed star (pentagram) represents the human body and the earth. In combination, the star surrounded by the circle represents the human body surrounded by the protection of the God/Goddess force. The pentacle is the symbol for Universal Wisdom.

9. Witches do concern themselves with Ecology..."[1]

This is **exactly** the same kind of PR I used to employ fifteen years earlier. While I was telling students and TV interviewers that witches do not worship Satan, *I was a Satan-worshiper!* It makes one wonder if the "woman doth protest too much." Let's look at a few of these points:

Witches Do Not Do Evil

First of all, the Bible declares that "**ALL** have sinned and come short of the glory of God." (Romans 3:23) That shoots that one down. Witches are sinners, just like everyone else. However, as I pointed out in chapter one, the witches idea of "harm" and "evil" is a bit fuzzy around the edges.

Secondly, what is this "Universal Law?" Where

did it come from? Who wrote it? By whose
authority is it promulgated? You will notice
that Ms. Cabot is also rather fuzzy about her
"deity structure." Other than assuring us that
Satan is not in it, and something referred to as
"God/Goddess" is in it, we know nothing of her
idea of deity.

What good is a Universal Law that comes from
nowhere? And if it comes from somewhere,
where does it come from? I know where the *"An
it harm none..."* statement comes from — the
Gardnerian/Alexandrian *Book of Shadows* —
but we have found that satanist Aleister
Crowley helped write that! His command, *"Do
what thou wilt shall be the whole of the law"* is
quite similar. Again, we are left to ponder the
source of these gnomic statements.

If you got a traffic ticket from your milkman,
would you honor it? Of course not, because he
had no authority to give you a ticket. Similarly,
what is the source of the authority of this
"Universal Law?"

Beyond that, who exactly determines what is
evil and harmful? For example, in my heyday as
a witch, marijuana was extolled as totally
harmless and an excellent way to develop
psychic powers. Indeed, the coven "pushers" of
pot were the celebrities in our little coven
society. Yet now we are learning that pot
destroys chromosomes, causes cancer, and also
fries your brain cells. Was it therefore wrong to
sell dope? We thought pot pushing was a

53

"victimless crime" but we were **gravely** wrong!

What about magic? As I mentioned in my own story, the ethics get a bit nebulous when you decide if you're going to heal someone without their permission, or do a love spell on a person without their knowledge. You see, this is all so vague it is meaningless. Suppose you have a relative with Alzheimer's disease. Would it be alright to put a spell on him to kill him and "put him out of his misery?"

Some witches would say yes, others would say no. To whom do we turn to settle these things? In some older witch traditions, being a homosexual was a "no-no," yet other newer witch groups celebrate "gayness." Did they get a direct line from the "Universal Law" to change the rules? Is it alright to cheat on your "lady?" If she doesn't know, she isn't harmed, is she? You see how misguided and useless this kind of ethical system is? It allows for all manner of exploitation and evil, and believe me – I knew some awfully selfish and exploitative "Wiccans" in my day. One of them stole my high priestess' wedding and engagement rings!

Then we have the "Three-Fold Law of Return." This is a concept related to Karma (see chapter on Reincarnation for more on Karma). It is one of the most widely taught and held ethical beliefs in modern Wicca. It is the belief that whatever you "receive" you are allowed to return it three-fold.

This "law" applies to both good and evil. It is so important that it is taught in the High Priesthood initiation in at least the Gardnerian/Alexandrian branches of Wicca, one of the largest and most established forms of the Craft in the West. In the initiation, the High Priesthood candidate has just been ceremonially scourged[2] and sworn. He or she is then requested to demonstrate their proficiency with the working tools of the Wicca.

When the ceremonial Cords are used, the new High Priestess (or Priest) is told to use them to properly tie up the initiator.[3] Then she (he) hears the following speech:

> For learn that in the Wicca thou mayest ever give as you receive it, but ever triple. So where I gave thee three (scourgings), return nine. Where I gave thee seven, return twenty-one. Where I gave thee nine, return twenty-seven. Where I gave thee twenty-one, return sixty-three. Use 9-21-27-63. This equals one hundred and twenty in all. (Initiate scourges High Priestess 120 times, then she says) Thou hast obeyed the Law. But mark well, when thou hast received good, so art thou equally bound to return good three-fold.[4]

What this means in practice is that if someone gives you five dollars, you, as a good witch, should feel obligated to give them fifteen. It obviously can also mean that if someone punches you in the mouth, you should punch him three times! Where this begins to torpedo Ms. Cabot's claim that witches do not do evil or harm is the fact that most witches are most likely to invoke this law in the sense of doing spells for vengeful purposes.

For example, if you perceive that someone has injured you in some fashion, either magically or physically, you have the "right" by Witch Law to hurt him three times worse. What often happens is that witches are injured in some real or imagined way and believe they have the right to hex the offending person three times worse!

In one city where we had covens, there was a fellow who was moving in our circle of friends but was not a witch, just a "hippie." He was in the habit of taking up with young girls, feeding them a line and getting them to have sex with him. Then he would treat them like dirt and dump them. He did this to a friend of one of the priestesses in the group, so she came to me and asked if something could not be done. I did a ritual and the guy was cursed with impotence. The last I heard, he still was impotent! Now was he hurt? Evidently. Did he deserve to be harmed in that way? Maybe, but for years and years??

Another example was a woman who happened to be staying with one of the priestesses in my coven. She was supposedly a friend and a witch sister. However, she ended up stealing all of the priestess' witch jewels. Again, we did a rite and invoked the Three-fold Law of return and the woman (who was not even 18 years old) chanced to fall down a flight of stairs and was permanently paralyzed — a quadraplegic!

We did not curse her and say, "Goddess, make her fall down a flight of stairs and be paralyzed." We just invoked this "Law" upon her. To end up a paralytic for life for ripping off jewelry is a bit severe. This was done when I believed I was a "white" witch and would never have considered cursing someone or seeking power from the devil.

I believed I was invoking my natural rights as a child of the Goddess. So for Ms.Cabot to write that witches do not do evil or harm is absurd, when this Three-fold Law is so commonly held to and practiced. Perhaps her particular group does not believe in the Three-fold Law, but if they don't, they are out of the mainstream of popular Wicca.

Consider the ethical implications of this belief. Our society would be in a constantly escalating series of either physical or magickal battles. If you rear-end my car, I have the right to total your car? If you kick my cat, I can kick your cat three times? If you rape my wife, I can rape yours three times? You see, this not only goes against the Bible's teaching, it goes against the commonly held sense of decency and morality of Western society!

We have a saying that "Two wrongs don't make a right." If this witch law was followed in terms of its negative side, our culture would disintegrate into an ever-intensifying series of vendettas,[5] a nightmarish version of a Laurel and Hardy movie where "You cut off my tie, so I can pour eggs in your hat." It is a monstrous morality which is most often demonstrated today in street gang violence and in mob "hits." With an ethical base like this, how can the typical "white" witch avoid doing evil or harm?

Witches Do Not Worship Satan

I call this "ostrich" theology. Ms. Cabot says that witches do not have a Satan in their "deity structure" (whatever that is). Ergo, he does not exist, right? Ostriches are believed to bury their heads in the sand to avoid trouble, like, "If I can't see it, it isn't there!" This is the unfortunate spiritual position of Ms. Cabot. She says because she does not have a place for Satan in her deity structure, he isn't out there, nor is there the tiniest chance that the gods or goddesses that *are* in her deity structure are simply masks for Satan.

Sadly, Satan is an inveterate party-crasher. He has no manners and will invade "deity structures" at will, especially if those structures have no place for Almighty God, which Ms. Cabot's deity structure does not. He will take worship anywhere he can get it, and will chew up Ms. Cabot and her deity structure for breakfast in the process!

Let's look at these resemblances between the typical Wiccan "god" and the figure of Satan:

1. Both are lords of death- and the source of death.
2. Both rule in an "underworld" kingdom of some sort.
3. Both represent bestiality and untrammeled lasciviousness.
4. Both are known as Lucifer in some circles.[6]
5. Both are believed to be the source of Light.
6. Both demand commitment by oaths and covenants.
7. Both seek to draw their worshipers away from the Bible's God.

It seems to me that if it walks like a duck and quacks like a duck, it's a duck, a very satanic duck. And if Ms. Cabot does not straighten out and repent, she may well find herself in the position of her hated *Witches of Eastwick,* cozying up to the Prince of Darkness himself!

Male Witches Aren't Warlocks

I can see why Ms.Cabot wishes to avoid the term "Warlock" at all cost. The word can be traced to the word for "traitor," "covenant breaker" or even "devil."[7] Although this is not a major point, it is something that needs to be dealt with, as it is all part of the "damage control" to their PR that witches like her are trying to pull off.

The venerable and authoritative OXFORD ENGLISH DICTIONARY[8] gives several definitions for the word, warlock, including: a traitor (c.1023); a wicked, damned soul, (c.900); the Devil (c.1000); the male equivalent of a witch (c.1560). The medieval compiler of witchcraft texts, Reginald Scot, uses the word frequently in referring to a male witch.[9] Thus, the usage of the term in this manner is at least <u>several centuries</u> old!

More significantly, the word *is still used,* both as a noun and a verb, at least among witches of the Alexandrian/Gardnerian traditions. Frankly, I am *amazed* that Ms. Cabot is not aware that the traditional *Book of Shadows* (which my wife and I received from our witch initiators in 1973 just "up the road" from her in Plymouth) reveals that there is an officer in the traditional coven, a priest called a warlock who is in charge of tying up the initiates for their induction into the various degrees. This ceremonial bondage is referred to by the verb "warlocking."[10]

So prevalent is the use of the word "warlock" that there was a major bookstore for "white" witches and magicians in New York City called "The **Warlock** Shoppe" run by major Wiccan figure, Herman Slater. After the outcry from his colleagues grew too great, he changed the name to "The Magickal Chylde," which is its name to this day.[11] Therefore, it would seem that either Ms. Cabot is trying to be unnecessarily coy about the present use of the word warlock, or she is woefully ignorant of an esteemed *Book of Shadows* from England.

Witches Do Use Spells

Big of her to admit it! Although some of what

she says is true, what she does **not** say is that spells, unlike the prayers to which she attempts to compare them, operate on the basis of a magical world view which implies that they are totally under the control of the witch.

In other words, the Christian or Jew always phrases his prayers in the context of the will of God (or at least they **should**). They acknowledge that God is sovereign and in control of the universe and that their requests should always be made in submission to His desires.

Witches, on the other hand, use spells believing that they are operating a sort of spiritual technology, like a cosmic vending machine. (See section below on "science.") The "Universe" or the gods are compelled to obey the witch if the ritual is done correctly. This creates a very dangerous moral distinction between the prayers Ms. Cabot mentions and the concept of the spell.

It is the ethical difference between asking God to relieve you of a repressive husband under whom you must live and going up to the man and blowing his brains out with a pistol. If Witchcraft is as scientific as Wiccans claim, then there is **that deep**, amoral distinction between praying and spell-casting; and if it isn't as scientific as we are led to believe, it is still ethically irrelevant.

Why? Because if you aim a gun at a person and pull the trigger and the gun does not discharge because you failed to realize it wasn't loaded, you are still guilty of the intention of murder! The court would still convict you of attempted murder. A witch who really believes magic works is morally culpable for the results she intends to achieve.

Witches Use Witchcraft as a Science, Art and Religion

I'll grant Ms. Cabot that Witchcraft is an art of sorts and a religion; but although it is ceaselessly presented as a "science," it is *not*, at least in any meaningful sense of the word. This needs to be addressed because it is witchcraft in its scientific window dressing which is now being foisted on our children in the public schools.

"Science" above all else implies empirically established repeatability. In other words, electrical engineering is scientific because we know that every time we turn on a light switch, a light turns on. A true scientific hypothesis must be able to be repeated as often as necessary and produce the same results. If you hook a light bulb up to a closed circuit and a switch, you can be confident that every time you turn on the switch, the light bulb will glow.

You can be secure that if you let your fellow scientist set the experiment up following your instructions, every time he or she throws the switch, the light bulb will light! That is science. We see its applications thousands of times a day in many things like automobiles, TV's and tape recorders — things we take for granted. We know that every time we push a button, click a switch or turn a key, an anticipated result will occur.

Witchcraft is not like that! You cannot open up your Book of Shadows or any of the common books on Craft magic and do the ritual with even a 50% confidence that the thing will work. I know! I presided over literally hundreds of rituals as a high priest, both individual and group; and watched many amazing things happen by the power of the "Old Ones" (demons!).

But I also saw just about as many times when *nothing* happened! You cannot guarantee that if you light your green candle and burn your jasmine incense and cast your water invoking pentagram just right (according to the instructions) that you will always have a successful harmony ritual. Without that "repeatability," what you've got is a superstition or religion of sorts, but hardly a science.

You'd throw out your TV if it only worked 50% or even 75% of the time — yet those odds are just as good, if not better, than the chances your magic has of working in any witch group I've ever seen.

You might ask, "If Wicca is so dangerous and is run by demon power as you say, why doesn't it work all the time?" The answer to that, my friends, is that there is another "Game" in town.

Jesus Christ is infinitely more powerful than the "Old Gods" of Wicca, and He can intervene whenever it suits His sovereign purposes.

For example, if a witch tries to influence a Christian believer with a magic spell, it will often fail to work, simply because the Lord watches over His children carefully. God will not allow the devil to touch them unless He has some higher purpose for letting him do so. Also, I know that at times the Lord Jesus interfered with the magic I attempted, probably because Christians like the lady I mentioned above were praying for me.

This is why magic can never be a science — because it is basically a game between the witch and the demons, who are the REAL power, her "magic" — a game in which the Lord God can intervene at any time, like a father who breaks up his kids' baseball game because it's time for supper.

The issue of what magic is and where the terms for "witch" come from will be dealt with in the following chapter, so I will skip over that.

Light Gives Us Wisdom

In point #8, a whole aggregation of metaphysical concepts are laid on us. Ms. Cabot talks about "the total intelligence refracting and reflecting all light." What on earth does *that* mean? Like much New Age and Wiccan mystical literature, it sounds like a bunch of enigmatic twaddle.

Intelligence is a quality of mind. How can it refract light? That is like saying "You can bounce a tennis ball off my emotions." Please, can we get *real* here?

She also says that "Light gives us wisdom." In the sense that we have to turn the light on to read or to find anything in the dark, that is true, but what sort of spiritual statement is this? Who or what is this "Light?" Is it the God/Goddess she mentions? Like many other occultists and New Age types, she keeps talking about this mystifying Light.

It is instructive to note that the original name for Satan was "Lucifer," the "**Light**-bearer." (Isaiah 14:12) The apostle Paul warns us that Satan can appear as an "angel of **Light**" (2 Corinthians 11:14). As has been mentioned earlier in the book, it is also important to note that one of the most common Wiccan names for their Horned God is Lucifer. We would be very cautious if we asked what the source of Ms. Cabot's "Light" was, and how she knows it is not from the fountainhead of all evil, Satan!

She may well ask, in turn, how we can know that it is the light of Satan, and not some altogether different being. That is not difficult to answer. Jesus Christ said:

> I am the *Light of the World*: he that followeth me shall not walk in darkness, but shall have the light of life. John 8:12

Elsewhere, in the same gospel, we read that Jesus:

> ...was *the true Light*, which lighteth every man that cometh into the world."
>
> John 1:9

A couple of verses earlier, we read:

> "the light shineth in darkness and the darkness comprehended it not (or "Could not overcome it")." (verse 5).

Now please note this. Jesus' Light is the ***TRUE*** Light, and it is a light which cannot be overcome by darkness. Now the light of the Wiccan "god" (whatever his name) waxes and wanes. It is overcome by darkness in the fall and indeed "dies," according to the central legends of the Wicca. It is then reborn in the time of the Winter solstice or at Imbolc (February 2). The Wiccan god is always subservient to the goddess, who is often depicted as darkness. Add that to the fact that witches do not have much, if anything to do with Jesus Christ, and you are left with only one logical conclusion.

If Jesus is the true Light and the Wiccan god is not reached through Jesus, then it stands to reason that the Witches' Light must be a false light. This is especially likely since the Bible also warns us against the worship of, or religious use of stars in Amos 5:26 and elsewhere.

Ms. Cabot and her colleagues can say that they

do not believe in the Bible or in Jesus, which is their right. However, what can they point to as another source of truth instead? A *Book of Shadows* of uncertain origin? An unknown source of "Universal Wisdom?" A mish-mash of legends with no basis in objective reality whatsoever? Their own "higher selves?"

At least the Bible has objective reality and can be tested. How can you test your "universal wisdom?" After sixteen years, I finally decided the Bible was more reliable than all the rest of this metaphysical obscurity rolled together! It gave me something more than mental "cotton candy." It was solid spiritual food! I spent over a year and half putting it to the test, and never found it wanting. Nor have I found it wanting in the six years since!

I think that you can see that we are dealing here with some very clever PR hype which carefully avoids central spiritual issues and which says more by what it doesn't say than what it actually expresses. In short, witches are learning to write like government bureaucrats! It is hardly a movement in the direction of intelligent discourse. As a witch high priest, I would not have stooped so low. If witches wish to live on the kind of ideological mind-pudding we have been discussing, that is certainly their affair. However, let them not call it "Universal Wisdom!" Frankly, it gives the universe a bad name!

3

What's In a Name?

or

Which "Witch" is Witch?

Recently, I was on a talk show discussing the problem of satanism. There was the requisite representation of Neo-Pagans and Witches in the audience. Fortunately, there was also a good number of Christians present, and some victims of satanic ritual abuse.

The witches, of course, vehemently protested that satanists, whether organized or isolated, *were not witches*. At one point, a Christian lady stood up to discuss Zeena LaVey, the daughter of Anton LaVey, and the current spokesperson for the Church of Satan. This lady referred to Ms. LaVey as a witch.

Promptly, from the Pagan side of the audience, a banshee wail, a literal shriek rose up, many voices as one: *"She is NOT!"* Whereupon, someone from another part of the audience cried back: "SHE says that she's a witch!" (Meaning Ms. LaVey).

This brought back a rush of memories to my mind. About sixteen years earlier, I had taken part in a similar contention.

An Early Confrontation

Mike Warnke was coming to Milwaukee to do a revival. Mike is a former satanist, now a Christian evangelist/comedian. In those days, (c.1974) he had just released his best-selling book, THE SATAN SELLER. I was living in Milwaukee, and was, at the time, the high priest of a network of covens. We had just helped incorporate a "church" called *The Temple of the Wiccan Rede*. When we heard Warnke was coming to town, we smelled blood!

We knew he spoke out on satanism in his meetings, and that he did not attempt to distinguish between "white witchcraft" (Wicca) and satanism. So we sent a telegram to Warnke, warning him that we (Wiccans) would be at his meeting in full force, and that if he made one remark about witches being satanists or devil-worshipers or anything like that, we would spring up and challenge him to a debate right on the spot — plus we'd probably sue him for libel.

So the night of the meeting we trooped in, perhaps fifty to one hundred of us, some in black robes and many wearing pentagrams and other badges of our Craft. We went to the only large block of chairs which was close to the front, right behind the section for the hearing impaired. That had a certain theological irony, for at the time, most of us were — indeed — *spiritually deaf!*

In any event, we sat there and glowered at him through the whole message, *daring* him to say anything slanderous about our religion — to accuse us of being satanists. For whatever reason, Mike did not say anything to that effect, although he did blast satanism pretty bad. I actually enjoyed his humor, since I had been expecting some grim, fire-breathing zealot with slicked down hair and a blue chin.

When the meeting was over, we all stood when they began playing hymns and stalked out, feeling that Pagan virtue had triumphed over Christian mendacity! Unfortunately, his message didn't seem to get through to me, at least *at the time.*

The only reason I recount this event is because of one interesting fact. While we sat there, so forbiddingly proud of our unsatanic rectitude, I know that I and at least one other member of our coven network were *card-carrying members of the Church of Satan!* In other words, our "butter would melt in our mouths" act was a hypocritical and insidious pretense.

As I sat in that audience, that memory forced me to wonder how many of those witches and pagans across the studio were really as innocent as they tried to appear, and how many of them were actually satanists doing a smoke screen to impress their disciples as I had years ago.

It also made me realize how ludicrous the entire issue of who was and who wasn't allowed to call themselves a witch had become. Since its inception in 1966, the Church of Satan has referred to its female members as witches. Indeed, LaVey even released a book for female satanists entitled, THE COMPLEAT WITCH: OR WHAT TO DO WHEN VIRTUE FAILS.[1] This was in 1970, some years before some of today's modern "Wicca" and Neo-pagan groups even existed!

LaVey's books are even full of mocking paragraphs about the "white witches" and how ludicrous such a position is to maintain. Of course, he had his own axe to grind. However, it is amazing to see how a religion as supposedly liberty-loving and anarchist as modern Wicca can erupt into a feeding frenzy when Zeena LaVey calls herself a witch.

As a witch, I met countless other witches, some of whom had valid initiations and training. Many did not — they'd just picked up a couple of books and decided to proclaim themselves witches. They were all very laissez–faire about the fact that anyone could be a witch simply by *saying* they were. They were very mellow and broad-minded about it. After all, it was the Age of Aquarius. *Anyone* could proclaim they were a witch.

Anyone, it would seem, except Zeena LaVey.

It is with this little argument in mind, that we

71

approach the issue of what exactly witches are, what they do, and where the word "witch" comes from.

This conflict began in the past generation with the emergence into the popular culture of the concept of the "white witch" or good witch.[2] Prior to the 1950's, very few people had ever heard of a good witch. The term was oxymoronic, like calling someone an evil saint. Witches were bad and everyone *knew* they were bad. We must remember that, for the vast majority of Westerners, there was no such thing as witches, outside of fairy tales and Disney movies. And that was the way witches liked it!

The Witch Next Door

However, with the legalization of witchcraft in England in 1951, subtle changes began to appear. The first major cultural effort in the U.S. seems to have been the immensely successful film, *Bell, Book, and Candle*; which starred all-American good-guy Jimmy Stewart opposite Kim Novak as a sultry platinum-blonde witch. The movie introduced most of America to the word "warlock" for a male witch for the first time. Although it was a fantasy; it served as a trial balloon for the concept of a "good witch."

This was followed by the British invasion of authors such as Sybil Leek, Gerald Gardner and Raymond Buckland, who began preaching the gospel of white witchcraft with a passion. Of course, the ultimate ground was gained with the popular TV show, *Bewitched*, which was basically *Bell, Book and Candle* domesticated and sanitized for TV. Elizabeth Montgomery's squeaky-clean, girl-next-door witch created a whole new image in U.S. conscious: the witch not as ugly old hag, or as vampy seductress, but as the sweet girl you'd bring home to mother.

It was about this time that we first began hearing about white witchcraft and "Wicca." We also began hearing emphatically that witches are *not* satanists and are not evil. We also began hearing that Satan was an invention of the Christian church and thus satanism was a Christian heresy which had nothing to do with the Old Religion.

Horror, Hype and Counter-Hype

The whole issue died on the vine as the hippie-culture waned in the late 1970's. Serious witches, like my wife and I, rejoiced in the disappearance of our religion from the spotlight; and we, like many of our colleagues, went back to our pagan devotions not really caring what the media was doing.

In the early 1980's, the New Age Movement (little more than technologized, yuppie-fied witchcraft) was moving to center stage, with our former witch friends quietly working behind the scenes. About 80% of the New Age concepts were lifted right out of witchcraft, but the media packaging was *critical!* It had to appear upscale, scientific and trendy. Thus the New Age took off.

However, the slumbering giant of Biblical Christianity was beginning to awaken to what was going on around it. Books were being written exposing the New Age-witchcraft connection! Then, the satanism media bombshell went off like a parachute flare over a battlefield and the witches scurried for cover like cockroaches!

There was the *Geraldo* show. Then, transcending even its hype, the numbing horror of the Matamoros drug/witch cult with its mass graves revealed in April of 1989. Suddenly, witches came to realize that some tar from these media brushes was getting on them. Serious damage control was in order, as all the years of Samantha's cute little nose twitch were being unraveled before their very eyes and being replaced with images of missing children and horrible mass graves.

The "Witches' League of Public Awareness" had been around a while, and they and other Pagan and Neo-pagan groups tried to reclaim lost media ground.[3] Laurie Cabot, head of the WLPA, first attacked the movie *The Witches of Eastwick* as a bigoted smear on witches, and reiterated the hoary canard that witches **do not** worship the devil or curse people. Then she began threatening the media during the Matamoros tragedy not to call the people involved witches or she would sue them.

"Those Who Control The Present, Control The Past..."

What this all amounts to is an attempt to regain the media "high ground." Witches like Laurie Cabot know all too well that for thousands of years witches were regarded, at best, as weird and frightening — and at worst, diabolically dangerous! They do not wish to return to those days and relinquish all the respectability they have gained because of a few nasty movies and some missing children!

They realize that they are in a position to rewrite history, *if we let them!* As Orwell put it in **1984**, "those who control the present, control the past; and those who control the past control the future." They know that if they can get their revisionist view of religious history into the school books (and they already have in many cases) and into historical texts, within a few years people will forget that witches were ever anything but wonderful nature-worshippers, skipping through the woods gathering herbs and singing hymns to the sun.

However, let us examine what a witch really is, and was, historically; and see if Ms. Cabot and her sisters can really pull it off.

What Were Witches Like?

Language can be a very tricky thing, but it often reveals a great deal about the anthropology of a question. Since we have established that the

Bible regards witchcraft as an abomination, let us turn to history and see how witches were regarded before the current PR blitz.

As mentioned elsewhere, the word witch and Wiccan both derive from the archaic word, *wicce*. Witches assert this means "wise one," but actually it derives from the root *wican*, which means to bend, and which hearkens further back to the root it shares in common with the word *wikke* (meaning "bad" or "wicked") and with the Old English word, wicca, for "wizard" or "wicked one."[4] This is not a very auspicious beginning.

We find that the earliest surviving record extant of the use of the word wicca in the LAWS OF ÆLFRED, (c.890) in which there are statutes enacted against such people.[5] From country to country and culture to culture we find little difference. The words translated as "witch" such as *venifica, bruja, stregoi,* or *hexenmeister,* all have evil connotations, meaning things like "one who curses," "troubler," "frightener," or "one who hurls curses."

In other words, it does seem that in most ancient cultures, to be a witch was to be someone loathed, feared and even hated. Even Anton LaVey notes that:

> "Anthropologists have shown that even in primitive societies, notably the Azande, the definition of *witch* carried negative connotations."[6]

Note please that these cultures are *not* "contaminated with Judeo-Christian prejudices" against witches. Even the typical *pagan* feared and mistrusted witches. To this day, most dictionaries will associate the word "witch" first and foremost with black magic. For example:

> 1. a person, now esp. a woman, who professes or is supposed to practice magic, esp. **black magic or the black art.**[7]

WEBSTERS', probably the most widely used dictionary in the U.S., defines a witch as a woman supposedly possessing magic powers, gained by "...a compact with the devil or evil spirits."[8] Another popular dictionary also connects the power of witchcraft with evil spirits![9] You can see how far this is from the simpering witch-next-door image of TV!

Even the popular film culture fights against this kind of stereotyping. The number of films with evil witches of one sort or another is legion, not that those should be taken as gospel truth, but they do indicate that in spite of twenty years of indoctrination, most people world-wide, think of witches as evil.

Playing Word Games?

However, words are slippery, especially in this culture where "gay" has ceased to mean happy and taxation has become "revenue enhancement." We musn't let this one slither out from under us!

Ms. Cabot calls it slanderous to identify the killers in Mexico with witches. But can she and her colleagues re-define a word which has been so long in the common parlance? Can they hide behind the shield of religious freedom which is so precious to us in America and tinker there with plain English.

She is trying to turn 4000 years of history on its ear by defining "witch" as simply a member of a Neo-pagan sect which does no one harm. Let us make an analogy:

Suppose someone decided to start the <u>First Church of Murder</u>. They put out slick flyers saying that Murderers have gotten a bum rap for the last couple thousand years or so.

They point out that the word "murder" might have come from the same root word as "mother" and that all members of their church are wonderful, upstanding members of the community who would never dream of hurting a fly. They issue their statement of beliefs, and lo and behold, members of the Murderers' church are pacifists and even vegetarians! They emphatically *do not* believe in shedding blood for whatever reason!

Now along comes Dan Rather and refers to some convicted criminal as a murderer on national TV. The legal department of the Church of Murder is up in arms and threatens to sue CBS for defaming a decent, legally-registered religion! Why everyone knows that Murderers are vegetarians and militant pacifists!

This sounds silly to us, but the position taken by Laurie Cabot and her fellow witches is just as extreme. They think they can undo millennia of history with a few tracts and books! And they are *wrong!*

Perhaps The Majority Rules?

We must also remember not to be too ethnocentric about this either. Most of these discussions center around Anglo-American witchcraft, or at best European witchcraft. *There are witches in every culture on earth*, and most of them are not at all shy about being called evil! Even here in this hemisphere, most practitioners of folk magic like Voodoo or Santeria acknowledge that one must learn black magic and demonology in order to do "good" magic.[10]

In fact, we must acknowledge that for every American or European Wiccan who insists that he or she is a "good" witch and there are no devil-worshiping witches, there are probably a hundred witches in South America, Asia or Africa who cheerfully acknowledge their utter dependence on evil spirits or demons and some sort of evil "god."

Thus, it comes down to which witch we are going to allow to define their faith for them. A comparative handful of Neo-pagans (a couple of hundred thousand, at most) or the legions of witch doctors, shamans, etc. who daily traffic in demons?

It would seem that both the weight of history and worldwide anthropological demographics stands against the idea of "white" witchcraft.

A Note of Caution

In the midst of this discussion, we must not forget a couple of key points. Many, perhaps most, self-professed "white witches" are in the same position I was in during the late sixties. They are falling for their own PR! Like any person in any false religion, they have accepted as true the things they have read and been told.

Being sincere, trusting people, they do not readily imagine that either the people over them or the spiritual powers in whom they have placed their trust would be anything but kind and truthful to them. They do not realize that perhaps their elders or high priesthood could be doing to them exactly what I did to my low level witches: concealing from them the real truth until they are "evolved enough" to deal with it.

As a result, they have not yet been let in on the deception, and thus they are victims, not fiends. However, they are still sinners and need Jesus Christ more than they could possibly imagine.

Most of them are not involved in any more illegal activity than perhaps using drugs; and few would approve of or consent to either animal or human sacrifice. They are honestly dumb-founded when people refer to them as devil-worshipers! I know I would have been.

It is important to understand that most witches, like many other cultists (Mormons, Masons etc.) are hostages of their own PR! Therefore, we must be as compassionate, patient and under-standing as possible, "speaking the truth in love" (Eph.4:15). We must explain to them that both the Bible and history declare them victims of an ancient and profound evil.

We must make them understand as well that we are not persecuting them, nor trying to prevent them from worshiping freely (as long as their activities are not anti-social). We are simply warning them of the danger in which they find themselves without Jesus Christ.

Should they choose to ignore our warning, we are not going to hang them or burn them at the stake, nor run them out of town. We will simply pray for them and tell them about Christ and the fact that He loved them so much that He died for them.

It is the same that we would do for anyone we love with the love that Jesus Christ gives us!

4

Concerning The "Burning Time"

Having discussed the real definition of a witch, it is appropriate to deal now with one of the thorniest dimensions of Christian-Wiccan dialog, what witches call the "Burning Time," a time of several centuries when witches were burnt at the stake, allegedly by the Christian church.

There was indeed a period in the Middle Ages of considerable savagery when being a witch was cause for torture, confiscation of property, and death by either burning or hanging. Although reliable figures are impossible to come by, it is evident that hundreds of thousands of witches or alleged witches were killed during the time of the Inquisition.

Currently, the witchcraft community attempts to hurl the charges of genocide and persecution against the Christian church and use those charges to somehow elevate themselves to the status of a martyred community. In other words, they try to lay a "guilt trip" on Christians as a strategy to procure favorable treatment, and to prevent Christians from evangelizing or opposing them. It also serves as a counter-charge when the issue of sacrifice and child abuse comes to the fore.

The reason this issue relates to the problem of labels is the fact that, horrible as this historical holocaust is, it cannot fairly be laid at the door of the Christian faith. This strikes right at the heart of the genuine definition of a *Christian.*

First, contrary to the general perception among Pagans, a Christian is not necessarily a member of a denomination or organized religious body. Rather it is someone who trusts in the Lord Jesus Christ to save him from his sins and bring him into fellowship with God. Thus, as is often said, it is not a matter of "religion" but "relationship."

Second, a Christian is one who *manifests* the fruit of that relationship with Jesus by obeying the commandments of God as we have them in the Bible, *evidencing the fruits of the Spirit* — love, joy, peace, longsuffering, gentleness, goodness, faith, meekness and temperance. (Galatians 5:22-23).

What Did Jesus Teach?

This means that not everyone who claims to be a Christian is one. In fact, the founder of the Christian faith, Jesus Christ, warned that:

> By their fruits shall ye know them. Not
> everyone that saith unto me, Lord, Lord,
> shall enter into the kingdom of heaven;
> but he that doeth the will of my Father
> which is in heaven.   Matthew 7:20-21

Earlier Jesus warned about wolves who come in sheep's clothing. That metaphor refers to someone who *externally* claims to be a Christian, but internally is something altogether different.

Mind you this is not the statement of some <u>recent</u> committee formed in the last generation to define Christianity. This is not the result of some human pronouncement. This is straight from the mouth of the founder of Christianity two thousand years ago! I am not making this up arbitrarily!

On the other hand, the concept of Wicca and statements like those contained in the Witches' League for Public Awareness literature are relatively recent and arrived at through a sort of consensus among various American Pagan groups. Even then, there are **large** blocks of witches, even in the U.S., who do not agree with it. Therefore, there is a considerable difference between the historical momentum behind the two attempts at definitions.

Pagan or Christian?

When we apply the two criteria mentioned above to the people who were burning or hanging witches, it becomes evident that they were certainly far from Christianity at least in the area of their discernable fruits.

By and large, the vast majority of the executions for witchcraft were done by the Roman Catholic church, which is not really an orthodox Christian institution, since it denies most of the cardinal doctrines of the New Testament.[1] This church does not teach the first tenet of the Christian faith, that a person can be saved solely through trusting in Jesus and making Him the Lord of their life. It has also not evidenced, through much of its history, many of the fruits of Kingdom living. This shoots it down on both points!

The Roman church is <u>far closer</u> to Paganism than it is to Christianity. Even many Pagans have noticed the resemblance. Many witches have sought out the Roman priesthood as part of their magickal development.[2]

Sloppy Syncretism

It is interesting how effortlessly the Catholic can slide into Pagan practices. For example, I would venture to say that about 95% of the nearly 200 witches we initiated were raised Catholic. The robes, the drama, the candles and incense were powerfully resonant to them of the faith of their birth.

This is even more true in Third World countries, where totally Pagan magical religions like

Voodoo, Macumba and Santeria can effortlessly blend African gods and goddesses like Erzulie with Catholic devotions to Mary. The result, in virtually all non-Protestant nations, is a bizarre syncretism which is both Biblically nonsensical and spiritually dangerous. If Catholicism is Biblical Christianity, then how can it meld so easily with Pagan cults? Let's see how:

A Pagan Checklist

What does the Roman church have in common with modern Paganism?

1. Both teach "salvation" through ritual acts and good works.
2. Both have a god and a goddess (Mary) figure in their pantheon.
3. Both have a slain and risen god who dies and is reborn in a seasonal cycle of ritual dramas.
4. Both have magic or thaumaturgy (Transubstantiation in the Mass) as central elements in their theology.
5. Both make extensive use of incense, statues, candles and ceremonial robes in their devotions.
6. Both believe in a kind of second chance after death (Purgatory).
7. Both believe the rituals of the living can affect the dead.[4]
8. Both believe in rituals of pain and mortification for purification.[5]

It was the last doctrine which <u>ultimately</u>

erupted into the concept of burning witches in the Roman church. The Inquisition, which initiated the practice of burning witches, was a creature of the Vatican and it was used as an instrument to punish and destroy not only witches, but also "heretics." These heretics were frequently *Bible-believing Christians* who rejected the false doctrines of Rome and *did* believe one could be saved simply by faith in Jesus' sacrifice on the cross. This was true both before and after the Reformation.

So, ironically enough, it was often possible for an accused witch and a Protestant to be burned side by side in blazes kindled by the Roman church![6] Many of the accused "witches" were actually Bible-believers who died horribly **with confessions of faith in Jesus Christ on their lips**. Some of the greatest men to defend the Bible and fight for its translation into the tongue of the common people were thus murdered — men like Hus and Wycliff! Although most witches have never heard the stories of these men, their stories are as moving and heartbreaking as any trials and executions of witches.

Contrary to the Teaching of Jesus!

We must understand that the tactics of the Inquisition (and yes, sadly at times, of its Protestant counterpart) are <u>totally contrary</u> to the clear teaching of the founder of Christianity and the true and only Head of the Christian church, Jesus Christ! *Nowhere* did Jesus or the apostles of the New Testament command or even condone the torture or murder of non-Christians or heretics.

To the contrary, gentleness and love are the emphasis![7] Jesus said that "by their fruits shall ye know them" (Matt.7:20). The apostle James warned:

> Can a fig tree...bear olive berries? either a vine, figs? so can no fountain both yield salt water and fresh.   James 3:12

John the Beloved also wrote:

> If a man say, I love God, and hateth his brother, he is a liar: for he that loveth not his brother whom he hath seen, how can he love God whom he hath not seen?
> 1 John 4:20

By these standards, therefore, the men who spread hatred, and tortured and murdered witches, *were not Christians.* If by chance they were, they were acting in a **horribly sinful manner** — regardless of which church they belonged to. It must be admitted that some of the early reformers like Luther and Calvin condoned the execution of heretics and unbelievers like witches. This was a grievous evil, but we must remember that they were very much products of the Roman church in their training and their upbringing; and it took generations for some of the bizarre doctrines to be sifted out of the Reformed churches.

There <u>was</u> hanging of witches in America at Salem, and done by Puritans, but there was a great deal of hysteria around the Salem trials. Nevertheless, for these atrocities, these misguided Christian leaders would have to answer before the judgement seat of Christ; and we, as Christians must admit these wrongs. However, Salem was one of the last "gasps" of this kind of detestable practice; and the stronger the sway the Bible held over America and even Europe, the less frequently witch persecutions occurred. The only places where witches have been burnt in the last couple centuries have been in countries totally in the grasp of the Vatican!

Will the
<u>REAL</u> Christians
Please Stand Up?

The bottom line in this discussion is that although fiendish things were done to witches and heretics in the name of Jesus Christ, they would *never* have been approved by Jesus! Where atrocities were committed, they were committed by men totally sold out to an **unbiblical** system of salvation by works who were probably not even Christian. At best, they were misguided Christians who were reacting in a sinful manner contrary to the teaching of Jesus.

"Thou Shalt Not Suffer a Witch to Live..."

Doubtless, some of my Pagan readers are sitting

up in their chairs and thinking angrily, "But doesn't the Bible teach that 'thou shalt not suffer a witch to live'? That sounds pretty much like a mandate from your God to kill witches!" Indeed, the Bible does teach that, but in the Old Testament, in Exodus 22:18.

However, anyone, Christian or Pagan, who tries to apply that verse today is misusing the Bible. Our Pagan readers will doubtless say, "Don't you Fundamentalist types believe every word of the Bible to be the Word of God?" Yes, we do; but as is often said, a text without a context is a pretext!

That passage is part of the Old Testament law, also known as the Law of Moses or the Mosaic Law. In fact, it appears just a couple of chapters after the famous scene of the giving of the Ten Commandments to Moses in Exodus 20. It is part of an exacting code of rules given by the Lord God to the Israelite people which was basically designed to confront them with their own inability to be perfect without His help. Even in the Old Testament, God made it plain that the Law of sacrifices was not His heart's desire for Israel, but something necessary although provisional. He said through His prophet, Hosea, for example:

> For I desired mercy and not sacrifice;
> and the knowledge of God more than
> burnt offerings.   Hosea 6:6

Trainer Wheels

As the Apostle Paul explains in the New Testament:

> Wherefore, the Law was our *schoolmaster* to bring us unto Christ, that we might be justified by faith.
>
> Galatians 3:24

The word there "schoolmaster" in the original Greek is the root of our word "pedagogue," but in Paul's day and culture, it did not mean a teacher or principal; it meant a servant who was hired to walk the child to school and make certain he got there safely and on time.

A more modern version of what Paul is teaching here would be that the Mosaic law was like a child having trainer wheels on his bicycle, to help him along until he got good enough to ride without them. The Law, like those wheels, was there because of weakness and immaturity; but were never intended by the Lord to be a permanent feature of His covenant peoples' lives.

The New Testament reveals that Jesus *abolished* that code when He died on the cross. Jesus Himself taught: "For all the prophets and the law prophesied until John (the Baptist)" Matt.11:13.

Elsewhere, John the Evangelist and Apostle tells us: "For the law was given by Moses, but grace and truth came by Jesus Christ." (John 1:17)

Paul writes even more clearly:

> (Jesus) blotting out the **handwriting** of **ordinances** that was against us, which was contrary to us, and took it out of the way, nailing it to his cross; and having spoiled principalities and powers, he made a show of them openly, triumphing over them in it.   Colossians 2:14-15

Elsewhere, the same Apostle writes:

> But now in Christ Jesus ye who sometimes were far off are made nigh by the blood of Christ. For he is our peace... having **abolished** in his flesh the enmity, **even the law of commandments** contained in ordinances, for to make in himself of twain, one new man, so making peace.
>   Ephesians 2:13,15

Does this mean that there is no more law? No more "thou shalt nots?" Not exactly, for God, through His Son, Jesus, replaced the Law that was written on stone tablets and given to Moses with a New Law, written on the hearts of those who believe in Him! Additionally, nine of the ten commandments are re-affirmed in the New Testament by Jesus or one of the apostles. The only one omitted is the sabbath observance.

The difference is that instead of the emphasis

being on external elements and rules and sacrifices, now the emphasis is on heart attitude and on receiving a new heart from the Holy Spirit of God, a heart which is not so inclined toward evil, but rather is regenerated or "Born again" by God's grace. God lives *within* the Christian believer! He makes it easier for us to do good.

A comparison might be made to a person driving a car on the freeway who is concerned about getting caught speeding. The Old Testament Hebrew was in that position. The New Testament Believer in Jesus would be like having a state patrol officer sitting beside you! Tends to make you more cautious.

An Age of Grace

On top of what has just been said, the New Testament reveals that we no longer <u>need</u> to live under the power of the Law of Moses, but rather under grace! Since Jesus took the penalty for us on the cross, we no longer have to worry about all those Old Testament punishments for sin, *unless* we spurn the free offer of Jesus' love and insist that we can do it ourselves.

If we do turn our backs on the cross, then the full weight of the Law comes crashing down on us. But even then there is no tribunal of elders or priests to condemn us. God alone will be our judge, and the verdict will still be the same as always: "The soul that sinneth *it shall die!*" (Ezekiel 18:4) However, that sentence is not carried out by any human being, but only by God Himself, who *always* judges rightly. There is no danger of a miscarriage of justice!

This is why most Bible-believers do not believe in following the hundreds of commands and penalties given in the Old Testament. We no longer put people to death for committing adultery or blasphemy, even though the Old Law commanded it. That is why we do not bother to keep all the elaborate dietary rules of the Mosaic law, commonly known as "keeping kosher."

Because of this, we no longer kill witches either! Nor do we kill false prophets who get a prophecy wrong! A good thing, or every psychic in the business would be dead! We live in an age of grace, and thank God in Jesus' name for it! Most Christian believers believe that the hundreds of Old Testament regulations no longer apply.

A Tragic Misunderstanding

However, there are and always have been small pockets of people who believe that God wants all the Mosaic commands still kept completely, or at least partially. Today, such people fall primarily into two "camps," the Seventh-Day Adventists and the Theonomists.[8] The second group, especially, though Christian, believe that they must bring back a government that would enforce every single one of the Mosaic laws.

94

In this, most Christians believe they are dangerously mistaken. They are basically repeating the error of the Roman church, which sought, and often achieved a total religious dictatorship. Under the Theonomists, just like under the rule of the Vatican, witches would be killed, as would adulterers, blasphemers, and homosexuals. This is *not* grace but a return to law. It is an attempt to force people to obey the will of God by brute force, and it is not what Jesus intended.

In following this line of reasoning, these people are moving toward the same tragic mistake which the Catholic church made in thinking it could enforce laws from outside rather than leading men and women to seek Jesus' help to transform themselves from the inside out! Believe me, beloved friends, Jesus' method is much easier and much sweeter!

Therefore, we can see that the application of the "Thou shalt not suffer a witch to live" text as done by people claiming to be Christians since the days of Jesus has been woefully out of line with His own teaching. It is in fact a serious abuse of God's Holy Word. God has already provided a perfect Sacrifice for my sins and yours in Jesus. He does not wish to see witches burning or hanging from every hillock.

God loves witches and Pagans enough to send Jesus to die, <u>just for them</u>! He loves them enough to share the Good News of Jesus with them, if only they would stop looking at the abuses of all-too-human Christians and supposed Christians and look instead upon Jesus Christ, Who gave Himself for them!

Guilt Enough to Go Around

In other words, the "Burning Time" occurred *in spite* of Christianity, not because of Christianity! No true Christian advocates the imprisonment or execution of witches; unless they have committed crimes. I cannot express strongly enough the sorrow I feel for the evil things done to witches in the past in the name of my Master, Jesus. But I also cannot communicate vividly enough the fact that for any witch to judge Christianity on the basis of those infamies would be a grievous mistake!

Obviously, there is guilt enough on both sides of the "fence," with the pagan Romans killing Christians for centuries, and with the horrors of the Inquisition and its Protestant counterpart. However, the witch executions were done in clear and total violation of the commandments of Jesus; while the sacrifices and other sins committed by satanists and (yes!) witches are part and parcel of the theology of Paganism!

An Entirely Different Agenda

I can imagine the cries of outrage from our Pagan readers right now, but you must understand that the historical evidence is clear: wherever Christianity and the Bible prevail, there is tolerance and a liberty in the area of religion. Look at the nations which either were, or still are, heavily influenced by Bible-believing Protestantism: America, England, Scotland, Holland, parts of Germany and the Scandinavian countries. These are nations where freedom of religion and thought has prevailed the longest.

On the contrary, look at the Pagan countries: India, China, and most of the Third World, which is either pagan or Roman Catholic such as Ireland. These are countries with little freedom, high illiteracy rates, often rigid caste systems with little chance of improvement.

Both great pagan cultures of the Classical world, Greece and Rome, essentially rotted from within and died. Although Greece never descended to the total and savage barbarism of Rome, it still did many things which sound abominable — leaving babies out on the hillsides to die, the glorification of homosexuality, pederasty and slavery. Of course, Rome's carnage is legendary and almost unparalleled in human history, until the recent events of this century: the purges and the gulags of (pagan) Stalinist Russia and the holocaust of (Catholic/Pagan) Hitler.[9]

Red Herrings

The bottom line here is that the issue of the supposed Christian burning of witches is a colossal red herring designed to keep the sincere Pagan from ever investigating seriously the claims of Jesus Christ. It is side issue at best, which has nothing to do with one's eternal destiny.

Understand that if the Biblical gospel of grace is true, (and it is) then it would be stupid for Christians to persecute or murder witches. If there is nothing either a Christian or a witch can do to secure that witch's salvation except for the witch to freely reach out and ask Jesus to be his or her Lord, then the murder of witches would be self-defeating, it would be sending them into a Christless eternity, cursing the very Name which alone could save them.

A Bible-believing Christian knows that you cannot "arm-wrestle" someone into receiving Jesus or put a gun to their head and make them do it. It is a matter of the heart and the grace of the Holy Spirit.

However, if you believe in the Catholic/Pagan concept of salvation by good deeds, the need to mortify the flesh, and that you can get a second chance after death; then persecuting and torturing people to death makes more sense. The Roman church really thought that by burning an "unrepentant" witch or Protestant, they could possibly keep them out of hell and perhaps spare them some suffering in Purgatory. "Repentance" (when it occurred) was usually exacted under torture or threat of death. Can you see how contrary this is to the gospel of grace?

The whole twisted system only works if you believe that rote ritual recitations and being sprinkled with water can somehow save you. A person who denied witchcraft and agreed to be baptized while under torture would hardly be a Christian by the Bible's standards!

Thus we see that the entire atrocity of the "Burning Time" emerged from a warped and paganized form of pseudo-Christianity which had no basis in the Bible. While it happened, it had nothing to do with the Good News of the New Testament that Jesus had done it all, and that because He suffered and paid the price for our sins, we don't have to.

The other side of this wonderful truth is that because the Lord Jesus has made eternal life so easy for us to accept, the result of refusing His offer is to spend eternity in a very real place, the lake of fire, which is reserved for people who have not repented of their sins and their witchcraft or sorcery (Rev.21:8).

That is a hard message to bring, and an even harder one to receive. But by telling Jesus that you do not need His sacrifice on the cross, you are letting yourself in for a "Burning time" to end all burning times.

5

Witches and Drugs

In many ways, those in the Witchcraft movement who have been trying to convince the media that they are model citizens in every way have been caught in a cultural time warp.

When the "Wicca" movement began to take off in the early 1960's, it was moving in a parallel course with a similar movement, the introduction of narcotics and psychotropic (hallucinogenic) drugs into the mainstream of American society.

Prior to this period, few middle-class Americans indulged in any drugs besides alcohol, nicotine and prescription drugs. Marijuana was primarily used by "Bohemian" and beatnik types and some jazzmen. Outside of certain anthropological and metaphysical circles, LSD, peyote, mescaline, and psilocybin (the "magic" mushroom) were unknown. Cocaine and Hashish were "artistic" and "high society" drugs seldom found outside those circles, and heroin was buried deep in the despair of the underworld and the ghetto.

However, as everyone knows today, these drugs became "with it" in the 1960's for a variety of reasons. The counter-culture of hippies and drugs blended seamlessly into the emerging Wiccan and Neo-Pagan movement, as recounted earlier in this book.

Thus, although the "official" or public position of leaders in the Wicca movement was that such drugs as marijuana and LSD were not allowed in witchcraft meetings, the behind-the-scenes reality was something altogether antipodal. Everyone understood the need for this difference. Witchcraft was just emerging from the sewers of history and needed to place as much distance as possible between its present and its past!

In short, its public relations image had to be impeccable. Many of us had established legal church corporations by the late sixties or early seventies — and a legal church could never afford to be caught promoting an illegal activity. If anything, many early Wiccan spokespersons went the "extra mile" and extolled temperance in the matter of legal drugs like liquor as well. In our first degree meetings, for example, we cautioned witches against drinking hard liquor outside a magic circle. We discouraged the smoking of cigarettes as well.

The reasons for these teachings were not so

much puritanical (God forbid!) as they were matters of health and what we called "psychic self-defense." Cigarette smoke attracted low level "elementals" and a person who was drunk in a public place had a weakened "aura" and was very vulnerable to psychic attack and infestation by elementals and "larvae."[1]

Getting High!

However, once we got into the second degree levels and beyond, the use of drugs became more open, almost necessary. Marijuana was used freely, both for social and magical reasons. The higher we took our people, the "higher" we took them as well. The use of drugs like LSD and hashish were common in the higher degrees, usually for "ritual" purposes.

In fact, my personal introduction to hard drugs took place at a meeting of the major Neo-Pagan central organization of its day (which shall remain nameless), where I was given hashish in the appetizers without my knowing it. It was the beginning of a ten-year involvement in illegal drugs which only Jesus Christ could totally stop. But remember, witches believe that *"an it harm none, do what ye will."*

Although the public position of most Wiccan leaders in the seventies was "My no, witches do not take illegal drugs." In actuality, illegal drugs flowed like water in every Pagan gathering I attended, both those I supervised with my lady and those we attended elsewhere!

We even had a priestess in one of our covens who was kicked out of the coven because it was determined that she was a "Narc." Oh yes, we were fine law-abiding citizens!

Gaining the "Sight"

One of the most common ritualistic reasons for getting "high" was to do what used to be called gaining the "Sight." This meant the development of some sort of psychic powers, usually telepathy or clairvoyance — ultimately involving the opening of what occultists call the "Third Eye." This is the Ajna Chakra,[2] a supposed energy center located between and slightly above your eyes — hence the name. It can be "opened" or energized by the use of hallucinogenic drugs, although there are other methods as well.

Let the witches protest all they like that they are "drug-free." They are whistling in the dark again, if not **lying outright!** Right in the "bible" of Wicca, the *Book of Shadows,* there is a ritual to gain the Sight.

In addition to recommending tying the witch up naked and having her kneel down and crouch forward into a kind of fetal position and be scourged repeatedly (a real consciousness-raising experience, I can tell you), the *Book of Shadows* also recommends in its list of incenses: "patchouli is best of all, and if you have hemp, tis better still, but be very careful of this."[3]

Patchouli is an exotic perfume, not a drug. However, "hemp" is a common word for marijuana.[4] Basically, the Wiccan "bible" is telling you to tie the person up and carefully get them "high" so that they can acquire psychic powers. I had this ritual done to me, and have, in turn, done it for many others; and it <u>works</u>. However, the dangers, both physical and spiritual, are enormous!

The Eight-Fold Path

Not only is marijuana recommended in the *Book of Shadows* ritual to gain the sight, but drugs are also extolled in the same book as one of the eight paths to magic which are part of the "Witches' Wheel" or Eight-Fold Path. Basically, these paths are:

1) Trance
2) Drugs, Wine, etc.
3) Music, Dance
4) Rites, Spells, Incantations
5) The Great Rite (ritual sex)
6) Scourging
7) The Cords (ceremonial binding)
8) Meditation.[5]

These are the eight recommended paths to "Realization." This means they are ways that witches are taught to grow and mature spiritually. While a couple of them are quite alright, depending on the circumstances, several are a bit kinky. The one which concerns us at the moment is the second "spoke" — drugs.

"The Witches' Wheel"
The 8 Paths of Realization

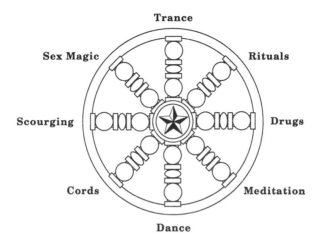

Again, please remember that this *Book of Shadows* is the ritual guidebook of the original "pioneer" Wiccan groups, led by Gerald Gardner. It is presented as the definitive guide for "white" witches, the very same ones who spent the last quarter century publicly denying any use of illegal drugs, and even "officially" preaching against them. Now the question becomes, which drugs are involved?

One of the first people to publish a complete and somewhat authentic *Book of Shadows* for the public was Gnostica's "Lady Sheba." She was one of several self-proclaimed "Queens" of the witches who started popping up like weeds in the mid-1970's. She achieved notoriety primarily because of her association with Carl Wescke's Gnostica group; one of the longer standing occult/witchcraft centers and a major publisher of witchcraft and astrology material under the title of Llewellyn.

Although her "queenhood" was never well accepted, and she has since faded into relative obscurity, her *Book of Shadows* is still around, and remains one of the few places to acquire an understanding of the Gardnerian tradition of Wicca's work book. In this book, she deals with the Eight-fold Path. Although the numerical order is different, the paths are the same.

She states, "The correct and controlled use of drugs (hemp, kat, mushrooms, etc.) ritual wines, whiskey...and incense."[6] She also gives recipes for witch's "flying ointment" which include opium, cinquefoil, belladonna, hemlock, and wolfbane juice.[7] She offers both an ancient recipe with some of these potent plants and ends by saying, "Mix with oil of your choice."

She also offers a modern recipe which is less bizarre (it only has belladonna and wolfbane juice) which she describes as "very amusing." She concludes by telling the reader to mix well and add your favorite perfume. Then she writes, "Aha! It seems as if we are not quite as tough as the old ones, eh?" Oddly enough, she adds a comment at the bottom of the page:

> "Most of these ingredients are psychedelic and produce hallucinations. They are poisonous and illegal. I have not used these, so beware."[8]

Are we supposed to believe that? Obviously, the comment was added because even in those free-wheeling days, Llewellyn's legal department probably got the shakes over the idea of producing a book which gave those recipes without a disclaimer. However, I think we are justified in doubting her sincerity. If she's never used them, how does she know that the one is "amusing?" Why even give the recipes if she tells us not to use them. It is like writing an article on how to build an H-bomb and then putting in a sentence saying how nasty H-bombs are and that we shouldn't build them.

The point is that witches were using hallucinogenic drugs! Our *Book of Shadows* had similar recipes, and we used them. But now, when drugs have suddenly lost their "trendy" quality, witches have had to begin doing some serious backpedaling to remain respectable.

The Way of Power

As if more proof were needed, some of the key books which had heavy circulation among Wiccans were the works of Carlos Castaneda. Books like JOURNEY TO IXTLAN, TALES OF POWER, and THE FIRE WITHIN, were purported to be actual experiences of the author, who claimed to be some sort of anthropologist. They involved his meeting with a Yaqui Indian sorcerer in Mexico named Don Juan Matus. This Don Juan became a major folk hero among witches. He was most of the Pagan movement's introduction to the idea of shamanism.[9]

Don Juan preached the use of powerful hallucinogenic drugs like peyote and mescaline to attain occult powers; and, according to author Castaneda, he achieved totally bizarre feats, including turning into birds, moving into wholly different "realities," astrally travelling, etc. Castaneda also supposedly ingested these drugs and experienced many similar adventures. The books, which are still in print to this day, are virtual text-books in the occult use of powerful and poisonous hallucinogenic drugs.

The Castaneda books appeared on the recommended reading list of The Church of All Worlds, a major Neo-Pagan organization of which we were members. Also the works of Joseph Chilton Pierce THE CRACK IN THE COSMIC EGG and Aldous Huxley THE DOORS OF PERCEPTION were endorsed, both of which deal with "alternate realities," mystical experiences and powers which can be achieved through psychedelic drugs. Much of the underground and published material circulating among the Neo-Pagan/Wiccan crowd throughout the 70's continually talked about drugs as the path to shamanism and power.

A Reality Crash

However, as the 1980's began the separate "realities" of these various shamanic disciplines within Wicca and Neo-Paganism crash landed on the desolate plains of drug addiction, suicide and madness. As people awakened to how dangerous most of these drugs really were, the druggie elements within witchcraft slithered back underground.

Even some of the major magickal drug gurus like Timothy Leary, Robert Anton Wilson and Baba Ram Dass began folding their traveling medicine shows and getting into "less dangerous" forms of mind games. Leary now designs software, Dass is even deeper into his New Age Eastern thing, and Wilson, their chief sycophant and press agent, now writes about libertarianism, the Illuminati and ceremonial magick.

All of a sudden, the shamanic/witchcraft idea that you could alter your reality or even slip into a different reality was coming up against a nasty and unalterable form of realism. Many of the witch leaders we knew had developed acute drug problems. That wasn't supposed to happen if you dealt with the "devas" or the group mind of the drug plant and became one with it. However, it was happening anyway.

Some of our best friends developed serious substance abuse problems, in spite of their devotion to the Goddess and their magical "maturity." We were being forced to wake up and smell the acrid stench of bondage all about us. Fortunately, in spite of a lot of heavy drug use, the Lord Jesus Christ brought me out of the occult and delivered me from all drug bondage! Some of our friends who relied upon the "Old Gods" of the Wicca did not fare so well.

The Tragedy at Matamoros

Now, years later, more and more evidence is emerging about the dangers of drugs. Ironically, the same media which ten years ago glamorized drug use now gives us 60-second sermons on TV about how horrid drugs are. NOW, after almost a whole generation of kids have been exposed to the garbage.

One unexpected element in the dark side of the culture which erupted on the scene in the mid-eighties was the incredibly vicious violence of the drug merchants, both among themselves and towards others. One of the most jarring events in recent years on that score was the formerly mentioned discovery of the mass killings in Matamoros, Mexico.

Headlines all over the country screamed, **"DRUGS, SATANISM, WITCHCRAFT CULT."** The hype of the *Geraldo* special was surpassed by the horror of these mass graves. In the midst of the clamor, I was interviewed on a Texas radio station. The host brought to my attention that Laurie Cabot, one of Wicca's most visible apologists today, had been complaining to the media about their use of the words, "drugs" and "witchcraft" in the same sentence.

I was told that Ms. Cabot declared emphatically that witches do not use drugs, and therefore it was rather slanderous to thus defame an innocent and legal religious institution. The host asked me for my thoughts on that.

I pointed out that as long as there have been witches, they have dealt in drugs, both of the medicinal variety and of the hallucinogenic and narcotic variety. I mentioned the use of flying ointments, marijuana, and fly agaric which had been traditionally associated with witches for centuries. I pointed out that even in the Greek Old Testament, the Septuagint, the word for witch was pharmakopaeia, which basically meant dealer in drugs and poisons.

I told him that virtually every witch I had known (and I knew hundreds) used drugs like they were going out of style, and that Ms. Cabot was flying in the face of thousands of years of history to declare that witches do not deal in drugs. Perhaps her little group in Salem is "drug-free," I certainly wouldn't know. I just know that to find a drug-free witch coven is about as easy as finding a Christian church without a Bible in it.

I sincerely pray that witches have cleaned up their act since I came out. Today's witches have better data on drugs than we did. Let's not let them get away with rewriting history on this issue. Hallucinogenic drugs are such an *intrinsic* part of the practice of witchcraft that I don't think they can get rid of the drugs without getting rid of the witchcraft. That wouldn't be a bad idea either, especially if they found Jesus Christ waiting for them outside the witchcult, as He has been for so long.

6

Due Sacrifice

or

*Who was that Goddess I saw you
with last night?*

One of the most charming elements in Wicca is
the way they present their concept of deity.
Their apprehension (which varies slightly from
group to group) of a godhead consisting of a
gentle Mother Goddess and a dark, Byronic
Horned Hunter God appeals to both the
romantic temperament and to the feminist.

It seems to have more of an "equal opportunity"
deity than the Father image of Judeo-
Christianity. Its anthropomorphic qualities
appeal as well. We like gods made in our own
image, who have sex and passions, who become
lonely or sad and that can grieve for a lost loved
one as the Mother Goddess grieves for her
horned consort.

Most often when witches are accused of being
devil-worshipers or satanists, they will deny it
by affirming their faith in a Goddess. This
Goddess is presented as a gentle, maternal
figure; with enough glamor and mystery to

make her transcendental. Again, witches like to contrast her with the God of the Bible, who seems like such a stern spoilsport by comparison.

While the Biblical Jehovah is striking people with thunderbolts as they step out of line, their Goddess plays and frolics with her hidden children, the Wicca. There don't seem to be any "thou shalt not's" in her vocabulary. She is everyone's fantasy idea of a mother or lover: a gorgeous, compassionate woman who loves unconditionally, does not chide or require much of you, and who is totally available for both service and sexual intimacy.

I fell in love with this image of the Goddess immediately. Upon reading a couple of books on Wicca, she emerged as the perfect being worthy of my worship. Her image stayed with me longest. I felt the greatest amount of holy awe every time I said her secret name in our Third Degree rites.

My notions of the Horned God evolved somewhat over the years, but my view of the Goddess remained quite constant. This very open-ended quality of the Goddess is one of her most beguiling features.

One Goddess, Many Names

Not that the Goddess didn't have her more forbidding side. In many ways, she was acknowledged as a projection of the love-fear relationship which men feel for women. Oddly enough, although Wicca is supposedly a matriarchal religion, its earliest modern proponents seem to have been men.

Basically, this changing dynamism of the Goddess is said to be related to the phases of the moon. Most witches identify the Goddess in three facets, relating to the waxing and waning moon. There is the Virgin Goddess (waxing moon), represented by a pubescent girl. There is the Mother Goddess (full moon) who is the pregnant mother. Finally there is the Old Crone or Old Hag (dark moon) who is the post-menopausal, but wise woman.[1]

Often, this third aspect of her is a bit weird and terrifying. The Crone is often associated with death. In our tradition of Wicca, which used names out of the Celtic pantheon, the Crone was called Cerridwen. We acknowledged in our traditions and rituals that the Goddess was known by many different names in each of her aspects. Yet all these were ultimately one Goddess.

In one of the central rituals of many covens, there is an invocation which begins:

> "Listen to the words of the Great Mother, who was of old also called Artemis, Astarte, Athene, Dione, Melusine, Aphrodite, Cerridwen, Dana, Arianrhod, Isis, Bride and many other names..."[2]

These names may be strange, for the most part;

but they represent Greek, Egyptian, Irish, Welsh, and French names for goddesses. Witches freely acknowledge that their Goddess is universally worshiped in countless pagan cultures world-wide, whether as the Amer-Indian Changing Woman, the Hindu Shakti, the Babylonian Semiramis, the "Immaculately conceived" Blessed Virgin Mary or the Obeah goddess Aida Oedo. This very global catholicity of the Goddess also appeals to many today. It is very "broadminded."

Because of this patina of gentleness and cosmic eclecticism, it is very difficult to take a critical look at the Goddess with a witch. It seems like you are setting fire to the beard of Santa Claus. However, there are serious problems with this whole Goddess business. It is evident that such Goddesses cannot exist in the same universe with the Biblical God, much as many witches would like to think that she can.

Of course, most witches don't care a fig for the God of the Bible, and that is part of their problem! However, before we look at the Goddess from a Biblical perspective, let's cut through some of the PR around her and see if she is really the sweet, though awesome, figure most witches revere so highly.

Which Goddess?

A hidden trap in this many names-one goddess metaphor is that many, if not most of the goddesses out there are not the sort of girl you'd wish to bring home to mother. For example, the chief goddess of the largest and one of the oldest pagan cultures on earth is **Kali.** She is the consort of Shiva and tends to kill her lovers frequently.

Kali is most often depicted dancing on the corpses of her lovers with a necklace of human skulls. She has been worshipped for centuries, perhaps millennia, by human sacrifice! The celebrated Thuggee cult of India and Nepal were followers of Kali who strangled their victims as an act of worship to their goddess. The recent horror film, *Indiana Jones and the Temple of Doom* gives a creditable, if sensationalized, portrayal of the goddess Kali and her worshipers.

Although the British attempted to wipe out Kali's cult during their control of India, their efforts failed. As recently as 1985, evidence of human sacrifice to Kali has been discovered, with hundreds of deaths being attributed to her devotees.[3] If all goddesses are one, can this be the gentle goddess of Wicca?

Another form of the goddess in ancient times was **Lilitu**. This Sumerian goddess made it into the western pantheon under a slightly different name, Lilith.[4] Lilith is a figure out of Hebrew cabalistic folklore who was believed to be Adam's first wife and who devoured her own children alive![5] She was later believed to be responsible for deaths of infants who perished due to what we call "Sudden Infant Death

116

Syndrome" today.[6] In spite of this goddess' appalling reputation, I personally found that a lot of Wiccan priestesses liked to take her name as a "Craft name" and were fascinated with her. A curious testimony to the harmlessness of Wicca's goddess.

A bit closer to home, the Phoenician goddess, **Tanit**, demanded an ever-increasing number of babies be sacrificed to her cult in the third and fourth centuries BC. According to recent discoveries by archaeologists in Carthage, animal sacrifices seemed to decrease, while infant sacrifices increased under the reign of the Phoenician goddess cult.[7]

Even in Greece, the goddess **Artemis,** whose name is even honored in the above-mentioned litany, demanded human sacrifice for her worship.[8] Another goddess-name from the list, Cerridwen, who was a Celtic goddess, also seems to have demanded human sacrifice by decapitation![9]

One of the most celebrated names for the Goddess in Wicca is Diana, the Roman goddess of the moon. She is often portrayed as one of the most beneficent incarnations of the Goddess. Yet, even a Jungian feminist author admits that:

> "...infant sacrifices were regularly performed in honor of, certainly, some forms of the goddess. It is recorded, for instance, that around the sacred stone

117

which represented the goddess Astarte, ***hundreds of skeletons of human infants*** have been found. She was the goddess of untrammeled sexual love and first-born children and animals were sacrificed to her."[10]

Please note that this is the <u>same</u> goddess Astarte who was conjured in the above cited Wiccan ritual invocation. Would you want ***this*** goddess in your magic circle?

The question needs to be asked, if the Goddess demanded such wholesale sacrifice of infants, adults and animals in the past, why has she cleaned up her act today? Or has she?

"The Youth of Lacedæmon"

Echoes of this terrifying carnage linger even today in the most sacred parts of the Wiccan ritual. The central feature of most Wiccan full-moon esbats (monthly feasts) in the Gardnerian/ Alexandrian tradition is a ceremony already alluded to, called "Drawing Down the Moon."[11] A key element in this ritual is the reading of "The Charge." This is sort of an affirmation by the entranced High Priestess of the nature of the Goddess and what she expects of her "children," the Wicca.

Although the origin of the The Charge is unknown, it has become one of the closest things that Wicca has to a "doctrinal statement."[12] Generally, it is a rather lyrical and mystical bit of literature. However, on the subject of this chapter, it gives mixed signals, to say the least. At the beginning of "The Charge," immediately following the above quoted litany of Goddess names, the High Priest says, "At her [the Goddess] altars, the youth of Lacedæmon in Sparta made **due sacrifice.**"[13]

A few sentences later, the High Priestess, speaking for the Goddess, says:

> **"Nor do I demand sacrifice;** for behold, I am the Mother of all living, and my love is poured out upon the earth."[14]

Here we have a problem. Witches love to quote this second passage when they find themselves accused of sacrificing anything. However, they do not linger over the first statement.

"The Charge" does not tell us what the "due sacrifice" was that the Goddess received in Sparta, but the late Wiccan leader from Great Britain, Alex Sanders, has revealed the nature of the sacrifice. The "youths" were candidates for becoming priests of the Goddess. To prove their worthiness, they were *castrated* and required to run up to the top of the temple hill carrying their recently severed organs in their hand as an offering to the Goddess. If they made it to the top without fainting or bleeding to death, their wound was cauterized with boiling pitch and they were made priests of the Great Mother.[15] (ouch!)

Obviously today, there would be few men wishing to become witches if this practice were being carried on. However, in traditional covens, it is still common for a ceremonial scar to be cut on the perineum of a male initiate.[16] This castration or scarring (called cicatrization) was fairly common in goddess cults of antiquity, as it symbolized a sort of artificial vagina which made the men (who lacked that particular organ) worthy to serve the Goddess.

Obviously, this is pretty grisly stuff, especially in light of some of the historical practices we have mentioned. Can we really believe that a Goddess who demanded "due sacrifice" in the past is not doing so today? With all the whipping and "suffering in order to learn" going on in the covens, I would say that the statement that the Goddess demands no sacrifice rings a bit hollow.

All we are doing here is presenting the fact that the sweet "Gentle Goddess" image that most witches are fed by their teachers is _not_ borne out by history. This Goddess has a bloody, savage and vindictive side which cannot be ignored, especially in the light of what the Bible has to say about her.

Ashtoreth

The Goddess first appears in the Bible by name in the days of King Solomon. Although he was noted for his piety and his wisdom, Solomon seems to have started to hang around with the wrong kind of women in his later years (around

984 B.C.). He married pagan women (1 Kings 11:1), which was forbidden by God, and they dragged their pagan gods and goddesses into the family with them.

The Bible records that:

> Solomon went after Ashtoreth, the goddess of the Sidonians, and Milcom the abomination of the Ammonites. And Solomon did evil in the sight of the LORD.   1 Kings 11:5-6

A couple of centuries later, the state of affairs for the kings of Judah and Israel were even worse! In around 740 B.C., King Ahaz:

> ...*made his son to pass through the fire* according to the abomination of the heathen, whom the Lord cast out from before the children of Israel. And he sacrificed and burnt incense in the high places, and on the hills and every green tree.   2 Kings 16:3-4

Just a few years later, around 721 B.C., we have this report concerning the people of Israel:

> And they set them up *images and groves* in every high hill, and under every green tree...and made them molten images, even two calves, and made a *grove*, and *worshiped the host of heaven* and served Ba'al. And they caused their *sons and their daughters to pass through the fire,* and used

> **divination and enchantments,** and
> sold themselves to do evil in the sight of
> the Lord.   2 Kings 17:10, 16-17

Although most witches know this, I should point out that Ashtoreth is an older form of the name Asherah or **Astarte,**[17] one of the names found in the beginning invocation of the Drawing Down the Moon ceremony. So again, we are discussing an important and significant "version" or archetype of the "gentle" goddess of Wicca.

We need to understand three things about these verses. First, almost all of what is contained in them describes modern goddess-worship: the rituals on high hills and under "every green tree;" the talk of worshiping the host of heaven; and of course, divination and enchantments, which are all part and parcel of modern Wicca. Divination is anything like astrology or tarot cards; and enchantment is magic spells.

Secondly, although some Pagan groups call themselves "groves,"[18] the term refers to an "Asherah pole" or an idol to **Ashtoreth** or **Asherah, the goddess!** Thus, we are hearing a report of the worship of one of the oldest forms of the goddess and her consort (in this case, Molech or Ba'al).

Thirdly, this "passing their sons and daughters through the fire" referred to a gruesome method of infant sacrifice done to the goddess and god. The idol representing the god had flames within it, which were stoked up and heated the idol's form to a scorching surface temperature. The child being sacrificed was placed in the blistering arms of the idol and burned alive! Is it any wonder that God forbade the Israelites from worshiping the goddess?

A Modern Counterpart

As repulsive as these practices sound, they resonate powerfully with the practices of Wiccan goddess worshipers today! Why is this? If they are drawing their water, spiritually speaking, from an ancient well with this kind of death and abomination polluting it, how can they help but become filled with the same kind of evil, no matter how good their intentions.

Although "white" witches and other goddess worshipers today will loudly deny that they practice infant sacrifice; all they have done is institutionalize and legalize the practice. You will find that Wiccans are at the forefront of the movement to preserve the right of a woman to kill her baby through abortion.

We ask ourselves, "What kind of parent would take their baby and fry it alive in the lap of an idol?" Yet our culture has accepted quite complacently the burning (with saline solution) or dismemberment (with suction) of babies in abortion clinics by the tens of millions!

As a witch, I was militantly "Pro-choice." After becoming Born again, I was led by the Holy Spirit to repent of such beliefs. As a new believer in Jesus, I was not surprised to find a coven of witches actively opposing the particularly strong Pro-life movement in my town. They showed up in their robes at rallies, etc.

I now find it difficult to understand the moral differences between the goddess worshipers of the past who offered their babies on the altars of Ashtoreth or Ba'al and the Wiccan goddess worshipers today who work vigorously for the maintenance of their right to offer their babies on the altars of the abortionist.

At least the ancient goddess worshipers killed their children out of religious piety, however misplaced. Today's Wiccans offer their children out of adoration to the twin "gods" of convenience and privacy.

We should not be surprised to see Wiccans at the vanguard of the pro-abortion picket lines. After all, the first abortionists in history were probably witches. As a witch myself, I knew of half a dozen herbal "potions" which could induce spontaneous abortions.

Bitter Fruit

Jesus warned that an evil tree could not bring forth good fruit (Matt.7:18). We have seen in this chapter that many of the ancient goddesses who are now being invoked in Wiccan circles were bloodthirsty fiends whose altars were drenched in the blood of thousands, if not millions! We have seen that, in spite of the utopian "Wonder Woman" image of the Wiccan goddess today, most of her early rituals involved human and even infant sacrifice.

You can't get apples off a hemlock or peaches off a wormwood, the Lord is telling us. If the root is poisonous, how can the fruit be healthy? If the source of the stream is poisoned, how can the stream itself be pure? We are seeing today the bitter fruit of Wicca's goddess worship in its anti-life, anti-family stands, in its anti-male fury against a God it perceives as its mortal enemy.

Can the modern Wiccan presume to domesticate this savage goddess and turn her into an archetypal lapdog? Can she continue to pretend that her "Gentle Goddess" would never ask them to hurt a fly? Many of them are already acknowledging a dark, untamed aspect to the goddess — and this admission has only come in the past 10-20 years or so.

Perhaps in another ten years Wiccans will be acknowledging what their more sophisticated colleagues, the satanists, have said all along — that the Goddess is more fiend than fairy, and that ultimately, she will accept nothing less than human lives ground to a bloody pulp upon her altars. They will see Isis without her veil, and discover Babylon, the Mother of Harlots and of all the Abominations of the Earth. (Revelation 17)

7

Is Satan Really a "Christian" Concept?

In the discussion concerning the possible satanic connections in Wicca, one of the common gauntlets thrown down by the Wiccan defender is the fact that "white" witches don't even have a Satan in their pantheon. The corollary to this assertion is the idea that Satan is a Christian idea, and/or an invention of the Christian church. Therefore, satanism, per se, is a "Christian heresy" having nothing to do with Paganism or Wicca.

This chestnut needs to be thrown out promptly, like the nonsense it is! Let us look at this notion and see if it has either historical or Biblical merit.

First of all, to say that Satan is an idea of Christianity is to neglect the literally **hundreds** of pre and post-Christian religions which believe in either "Satan" by name or in a Satan-type figure by another name.

A "Jewish" Devil?

The first, and most obvious example is the religion of Judaism, which is at least two thousand years older than Christianity. In the *Tenach* or Hebrew Bible (Old Testament), we have five "by name" instances of reference to Satan.[1] These passages were not written by Christian editors, they are in the *original* Hebrew Bible.

Interestingly enough, two of the instances are in the Book of Job, which is felt by many scholars to be the *oldest* book in the Hebrew canon of sacred scripture, dating from at least 1500 B.C.![2] That means the concept of Satan as an enemy and accuser of humanity is introduced in the first chapter of possibly the first book of sacred Hebrew writing!

Nor does Satan change much in his remaining appearances in the Hebrew Bible. He is always the enemy and destroyer of humanity, and especially of the Jewish people. Although many more liberal Jewish scholars today would not wish to profess a belief in Satan (nor would many liberal Christian scholars, for that matter) the fact is, he is in the Tenach, and for serious, orthodox Jews, he is very real indeed!

In addition to the above passages, a couple of other places where Satan is mentioned more indirectly are the prophets Isaiah (14:12-19), where we first hear the name "Lucifer," and Ezekiel (28:12-19) where we learn that Satan was a "covering cherub"[3] or Kerub, meaning that he was one of the most powerful angels who served to cover the throne of God Himself, and that he seems to have been in charge of the music in heaven before he sinned and fell into perdition.

In the Isaiah passage, especially, we learn that his sin was pride and wishing to be like God, perhaps to even overthrow God. This sin, desiring to become God, is at the core of both Wiccan theology and its handmaiden, the New Age movement. Most "white" witches either believe they are on their way to becoming gods, or are part of God/dess already, in a pantheistic sense.

Satan is also identified with the serpent who tempted Eve in chapter three of the **first** book of the Hebrew Torah, called *Bereshith* or Genesis. So not only does Satan appear in the oldest book in the Bible, but he also appears in the first book of the Bible, right after the creation of the world. That is at least 4,000 years before the founding of the Christian church by Jesus Christ!

Many of my dear Wiccan friends will say, *"Sure, but that's the Bible anyway. Jews and Christians are part of the same, monotheistic, sexist, patriarchalist mindset. It's six of one and half-a-dozen of the other!"*

A Pagan Satan?

Stunning as it may sound, there are also Pagan

versions of Satan. It goes without saying that *virtually every culture* has its concept of evil spirits. The classic and somewhat simplistic Wiccan is probably one of the few religionists on the face of the earth (along with New Agers) who believe there are no evil spirits (and many of them do believe in evil spirits).

Let's not play "word games" here. Every Tom, Dick and Harry witch doctor and shaman from here to Nepal believes that there are **legions** of evil spirits out there. Spirits who mean to kill, sicken and otherwise torment humanity! They may not call them "demons" or "minions of Satan," but that is how they are regarded. Most of these shamans are a blend of two distinct religious philosophies: 1) animism or pantheism and 2) dualism.

Pantheism is the belief that everything is God. Animism is the belief that everything (even "inanimate" objects like rocks) has a soul or intelligence. Quite often these two beliefs mesh together. A step beyond these two beliefs is **Dualism**, which is the belief that there are two supreme powers or gods which are opposed to one another and war with each other.

This is a logical consequence of a belief in evil and good spirits. If there are evil spirits, it stands to reason that they don't just hang out on street corners waiting to trip little old ladies. They must be expected to function in an organized fashion. Even street gangs have leaders! Therefore, there must be a "head honcho" evil spirit and a similar good spirit.

A Lord of Light and a Lord Of Darkness

The first apparent "institutionalized" form of dualism seems to be Persian Zoroastrianism, **many centuries** before Christ. (c.588 B.C.)[4] Zoroaster taught that there were two great powers, Ohrmazd, the good "god" and Ahriman, the evil "god." There was a great deal of influence upon the Jewish thinking from Zoroastrianism during the last centuries before the time of Christ in what Bible scholars call the "Inter-testamental period" between the Old and New Testaments.

It is important to note that many notions of both the Jewish heresy of qabalism and the Hellenic heresy of gnosticism emerged from this blend of Jewish and Zoroastrian philosophy, including the various "fake scriptural" books of Enoch, which are of significance in the development of occult demonology.

Please understand, though, that these were (and are) *defective* understandings of the nature of Satan. Both Zoroastrianism and the meanderings of Jewish thinkers were far away from what the Hebrew Bible taught. The cosmos is not a chess game between God and Satan! That is the <u>error</u> of dualism! It assumes that the Lord of Light and the Lord of Darkness are equal, but they are not.

God made **_all_** things, **_including_** Lucifer, the

mighty angelic being who became lifted up in pride and rebelled against his Maker. Therefore, God and Satan are not opposites or mirror images of each other. Satan's battle with God is like me getting into the ring with Mike Tyson. I would be powerless to lay a glove on him. And Satan was defeated 2,000 years ago by Jesus Christ on the cross of Calvary!

However, the point is that there are *countless* cultures where some form of Zoroastrian dualism is the belief system. All these traditions, whether tribal, aboriginal peoples or large, "sophisticated" cultures like the Parsees (contemporary Zoroastrians) believe in a mighty, supernaturally evil being who hates mankind and opposes God (or the "good" spirit).

And the Monists?

Even the "pure" philosophical monists like the Hindus often fail to live up to their monistic ideals on the grass-roots levels. A Monist, as mentioned before, believes that "All is one" and therefore there can be no evil. However, if you visit India or other supposedly monist cultures, you will find that most of the average people still believe in some sort of evil spirits which must be placated or guarded against.

Certainly, among the intellectuals and the higher castes, there are those who approach true Monism among the Hindu people. But even among them, when tragedy strikes those they love, they often find themselves seeking an explanation in the realm of an "evil spirit." This is because Monism is so contrary to reality and to the actual condition of humanity that it is a difficult belief to maintain "in the trenches." When your child is killed or your daughter raped, it is difficult to sit blissfully back and say "All is one" and "There is no evil."[5]

Thus, it is safe to say that a large majority of Hindus (c. 648 million) believe in evil spirits. Add those millions to countless numbers of people who believe in aboriginal magic or shamanism and you've got a goodly majority of humanity. Then we have the Muslims, over 840 million of them, who definitely believe in *Shaitan*, as they call him. Most Buddhists believe in evil spirits, and there are 307 million Buddhists.[6] When you add all of those people together and throw in the Parsees, Shintoists and Jews (none of them Christians) you have at least a couple billion people, representing several major world religious traditions of great antiquity.

It makes the measly number of Wiccans seem insignificant by comparison. All these various cultures have some concept of evil spirits and usually of a supreme evil spirit who is the origin of evil and the enemy of humanity. This puts the lie to the statement that "The devil is a Christian invention."

Ancient Devil Worshipers

Beyond that simple fact, there is the reality of

ancient, pre-Christian cults which worshiped a devil or Satan-like figure as their god! The deity best known because of his recent "press" is Set. Spokesman for the legal "satanic" community, Dr. Michael Aquino, claims to worship Set, and bases his "Temple of Set" upon his perception of the cult of Set (possibly the first male "god" to be worshiped[7]) which originated at least as long ago as the time of the VIIth dynasty of Egypt (c.4000 B.C.) and reached its supremacy between the XIIIth Dynasty (c.3180 B.C.) and the XVIth Dynasty.[8]

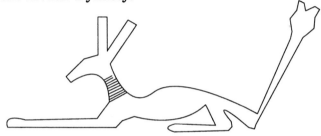

A hieroglyph of the Egyptian "devil," Set: ancient god of the Wicca

In the Egyptian Book of the Dead, this Set is hailed as having been first in order of glory.[9] According to one authority, he was "looked upon as the fallen leader of the angelic host because he had been the first in glory as the ruling power at the primary station of the pole. This is he that is worshiped by the Yetzidi in Mesopotamia, who say 'there is to be a restoration as well as a fall.' "[10]

Without getting into a critique of Dr. Aquino's

theology, suffice it to say that he has amply demonstrated the existence of a pre-Christian deity who represents evil (or, if you prefer Aquino's term, alienation and isolation from creation). According to Egyptian religion, Set murdered his brother Osiris and thus assumes a position analogous to Loki or Pluto (or the devil) in other mythological systems.[11]

Set's name may well be etymologically linked to Satan (the Egyptian Sht, leading to the Arabic *Shaytan,* leading to the Hebrew *Shaitan* and the Greek Satan). The very fact that Dr. Aquino left the Church of Satan and its founder, Anton LaVey, to found his own religion where a "real" deity could be worshiped rather than LaVey's "symbolic" Satan, should be indication enough of the reality of Set's cultus and his existence as a pre-Christian, possibly even pre-Judaic principle of evil.

The bottom line, my dear friends, is that Satan (whatever you call him) is out there and he is real. He was not made up by Christians as a boogy-man. He has been around since before the first human being walked the earth! He is an angelic being of the highest order, and is thousands of years old. That means he is both naturally brilliant beyond anyone's comprehension, and he has had millennia to study human nature. He is also, in the fullest sense of the word, a **psychopath** who hates all humanity with an unimaginable passion, chiefly because God loves us.

My point is, if we puny humans can come up with things like fishing flies and duck decoys to deceive and lure wildlife into our lair, don't you think it would occur to Satan to do the very same thing to us? He wants to blow us away, just as certainly as a duck hunter covets a mallard. And he has created a beautiful "decoy" to trick us.

A Deception with Eternal Consequences

The essence of a decoy is that it must look real and harmless. Obviously, Wicca appears real and harmless. However, it is based on a pre-supposition that there ain't no "bad guys" out there on the spiritual level who want to mess with a person's head. It is based on the (pardon the expression) naive belief that we can trust whatever spiritual information we receive, either from books or some inner, mystical prompting, as long as it is appealing and seems to make sense.

However, I ask you: What if that presupposition were based on faulty information? Your religious framework could be the most beautiful and logical edifice imaginable, but what if it is built on a faulty fundamental premise?

My dear Pagan friends, how long would you survive in society if you assumed that everything that was told you was automatically true, just because it somehow "resonated" with some inner sentiment? You don't believe TV commercials or the statements of politicians without first checking them out, no matter how appealing they might seem.

Yet here, in the most vital area of human existence, the spiritual and eternal realm, many Pagans and Witches are following the leading of books and/or "spiritual masters" with a lot less basis for trusting them than they have for trusting "Honest Sam the Used Car Man" on TV! At least the TV advertisers are subjected to scrutiny both from the law and from consumer agencies. Politicians are watched very carefully by the media.

But because of our precious heritage of freedom of religion in the U.S., there is no way to tell if a book you've bought on witchcraft or metaphysics has one lick of truth in it! There is no way to tell if the "leadings" you are getting from your gods or spiritual guides are true or not. You have been trusting them on faith!

How do you know they are who they say they are? How do you know that the Goddess is gentle and good? How do you know that the Horned God is not the enemy of your soul — Satan? The answer is simple: You don't! All you have is some inner, subjective feeling within yourself that it feels "right."

But if you are honest with yourself, you will admit that those feelings can be misled. Have you ever met a man or a woman whom you felt was just perfect for you, a real soulmate? Then the relationship turned sour? I'm certain that something like that has happened to you, because it is common in the human experience.

The high divorce rate in the U.S. shows that many people feel so strongly that they have found "Mr. or Ms. Right" that they have made a legally binding covenant to them. Yet more often than not, they were wrong! It serves to illustrate how easily we can let our emotions lead us astray. The Bible teaches us this as well. (See Jeremiah 17:9; Proverbs 16:25.)

But this is something even more important than choosing a lover or a spouse. This is choosing a "God/dess" to whom you will be wedded for all eternity. My beloved friends, if you die while in the thrall of the wrong deity, there is no chance for divorce or annulment beyond the grave. The choices you make here and now will determine your eternal destiny.

Is it really worth that kind of gamble? Consider the testimony of myself and hundreds of other witches who have learned that the god of Wicca is truly the devil and that he is a liar and a murderer! That is what Jesus called him (John 8:44). What reason do you have for not believing Jesus Christ, and instead believing Gerald Gardner or Miriam Starhawk?

Gardner is rotting in his grave, while Jesus is alive and reigning in power and majesty in my heart, and in the hearts of hundreds of former witches who now serve Him and Him alone! His power is so much greater than the "Dread Lords of the Outer Spaces." His track record over the past 2,000 years has proven that He is faithful and true.

Are you going to believe what your books and your Wiccan teachers have said about Jesus, or are you going to believe what He has to say about Himself?:

> I am the way, the truth and the life: no man cometh unto the Father but by me.
> John 14:6

What _real_ reason do you have to believe that Jesus is lying to you? What _real_ reason do you have for thinking the Wiccan God/dess is not really a beguiling mask for Satan? If you are honest, you will say that you don't have any.

Please do me a favor. Pray and ask the _real_ Jesus Christ of Nazareth to be the Lord of your life, and to reveal to you the true face of your God/dess. You have nothing to lose, and eternal life to gain. Take it from one (of many) who has done it, and is still praising Jesus for setting him free!

8

Is Reincarnation an Answer?

One of the pivotal beliefs of most witches is the concept of Reincarnation. Where this belief first became grafted onto witchcraft is probably impossible to determine. However, it is now an integral part of the dogma of most Wiccan groups.

Reincarnation is best known for being part of the ancient and pagan religion of Hinduism. Today, it is also believed by many outside either formal witchcraft or Hinduism, such as "spiritualists" and New Agers. However, in its purest form, it comes to us from the Hindu religion.

Most witches do not buy into the entire Hindu package, but only a Westernized version which does not allow for the transmigration of souls or "retrograde" Reincarnation. This classic Hindu version of the doctrine is that if you do evil in your life, you could devolve into a lower form of life in your next incarnation. Thus, a particularly vile man could be "reborn" next time as a rat, or even a bug.

However, witches and most Western believers in Reincarnation take a more positive view, and do not believe that a person can ever be sent back to an animal form, just into a less pleasant form of human life. This is called "Progressive" Reincarnation.

This brings us to *karma*, the key concept of Reincarnation, whatever variety. Karma is a Sanskrit word that basically means whatever you do comes back at you. Thus, if the nasty person mentioned above was a rich person who kicked beggars on the street and never shared his wealth with those less fortunate, he would be reborn as a wretchedly poor beggar.

A man who abused his wife might be reborn as a wife married to an abusive husband with no chance of escape. A person who killed or robbed might very well be reborn as an ultimate victim of murder or theft. In this way, the eternal scales of karma are kept in balance.

Of course the converse is also true. A good, noble person will be reborn in a better station next time around.

Where Does This Go?

The ultimate goal of this concept varies considerably from culture to culture. Some Eastern versions see the goal of this as a gradual move through lives toward perfection. When perfection is arrived at, the person moves off the "wheel of karma" altogether and escapes this treadmill-like existence and either merges with the divine (in some versions) or melts into the universe as a whole and ceases to exist at all. In other words, the soul's goal is *annihilation.*

In the West, and with most witches, there are subtle variations on this theme, designed to better appeal to our culture. Most witches believe that through your lifetimes you will gradually perfect and ultimately transcend the "earth plane" or this here-and-now existence. You will then become a sort of super-human being or "Master." Many witches believe you can ultimately become a god!

Variations on a Theme

Even within this westernized framework of Reincarnation, there are different nuances. Some Pagans, unsatisfied with the open-ended quality of going through an indeterminate number of lives down through the centuries, try to systematize the concept by fusing it with another occult system, astrology.

These people believe that you must incarnate at least once in each sign of the zodiac, thus a minimum of twelve lifetimes. However, if you blow it in your "Virgo" lifetime, you'll have to come back and be a Virgo again, until you get the "lessons" of that zodiacal sign mastered. This seems more manageable to folks. After all, you're only talking two or three dozen lifetimes.

A further variation gets into gender-bending.

The witch, usually a feminist, often adds to this equation the idea that you must experience a lifetime in each zodiac sign <u>for each sex</u>! You must go around once as a male "Aries," then once as a female "Aries." This just doubled the requisite number of lifetimes to perfection.

Of course, we cannot be racist; so some socially conscious witches believe that you must also experience the major racial types as well. You must be a Caucasian, a Black, an Asian and a Native American. Somehow this has gotten rather daunting! We are now talking about at least twenty four dozen lifetimes (288!)

Assuming you go immediately from one death to your next life (and there is by no means agreement on this!) and figuring an average of forty years per life, that means you're talking over 11,000 years to get it right! Even with the basic "plan" mentioned first, it would still take at least 1,440 years to perfect yourself. That means someone who is near perfection now has been at it at least since the sixth century A.D.!

Can It Be Done?

Before we look more closely at what the Bible says about this, let us look at this plan from simple common sense. Are there any problems with this program? Basically, four red flags go up at once:

1. The problem of getting rid of your negative karma.

2. The problem of memory and discipline

3. The problem of fatalism

4. Empirical testing

Most witches and Pagans are so attracted to the romantic elements in Reincarnation that they often do not bother to think through some of these problems in a rational way. I was this way myself.

I was told fairly early on in my occult career that I had been a medieval monk who had been walled up alive in his cell for practicing the esoteric arts (i.e. magic). I was so fond of this notion that I actually got an asthma attack while visiting a nearby monastery! Naturally this was attributed to past-life memories of suffocating within my cell!

Since most witches have a rather romanticized view of medieval or pre-Christian times, Reincarnation plays right into this world view! The fact that they feel somewhat "out of it" or alienated from their modern culture is explained by the fact that they are resonating to their past lives and are, in fact, quite "old souls." This is much more flattering than admitting that they might just be maladjusted or immature.

Let's step back and look at these issues objectively and see if the doctrine of Reincarnation will stand up to close scrutiny.

Negative Karma

This is probably the thorniest problem in the batch. Since witches and other Pagans do not like to deal with the problem of sin, they need to confront the issue of what is to be done with negative or "bad" karma. Basically, bad karma is just another word for sin, although the key difference is that your own "higher self" judges your "lower" or everyday self, rather than having some exterior being like God judge you. Thus, bad karma is anything which is contrary to your intended "evolutionary path."

Granting that the general concept of progressive Reincarnation is valid for a moment, let's look at what happens to bad karma. Progressive Reincarnation assumes that you start your first human life as a low-life, an "entry-level" human.

Let's say your first lifetime is as a bandit in some indeterminate land before the time of the Roman empire. You're running around raping, robbing and pillaging, building up scads of negative karma. You finally get an axe buried in your skull at the ripe old age of 30 and die.

You're reborn (for some reason or other) a notch higher on the moral scale next time around. However, you have all this negative karma built up from before. Let's say that instead of being a bandit, you're the wife of a shepherd. To help work off your bad karma, your husband gets beaten to a pulp by bandits. He's totally paralyzed and you have to support him by working in the sheep meadows while trying to raise five screaming kids.

Being a typical karmic low-life, a "young soul", you get really ticked off and spend the rest of your life a bitter woman, kicking your kids and sheep every time you have a bad moment; and building up still more bad karma like a festering sore. Now you've got two lifetimes' worth of bad karma! You see where this is going?

The Need for "Harmlessness"

Rather than carry this dreary example any further, let us "cut to the chase." The bottom line for karma is another Sanskrit term, *Ahimsa*. *Ahimsa* is the Reincarnationist's only hope! It translates freely as "karma-free" or as "harm-lessness." The key thing that you have to do is practice harmlessness.

What exactly does this mean? It means getting through *your entire life without harming anyone or anything!* (Remember witches are usually pantheists, which means that plants, rocks and animals are just as deserving of respect as people.) Can this be done? What does it entail?

Let us look at a Reincarnationist sect in India, the Jains. Jain monks try their best to practice *ahimsa*, I'll give them that! Wherever they walk, they carry a little broom and sweep the ground in front of them, lest they step on an ant. Of course, in sweeping the ant aside, they could

145

terrify it or damage its legs, but this is the chance you have to take when you're dealing with karma.

These monks wear masks like surgical masks over their mouths, lest they breath in a microbe or germ and injure it. They are (needless to say) the strictest of vegetarians, living only on nuts and fruits which, they say, are freely given by their trees and bushes, and thus can be received freely. When they bathe, which is as seldom as possible, they move very slowly and delicately in their bath water to avoid accidentally damaging one of the millions of microscopic organisms which live in water.

Since they will not kill insects, those who are wealthy enough pay a servant to spend an hour in their bed to draw all the parasites to their own bodies so the bed is relatively free of parasites by the time they finally take over for the night.

Obviously, this sort of life sounds utterly absurd to most of us, although we must grudgingly admire these folks' consistency. If anyone is going to make it in the karma game, they are! But even with these monks, there can be no guarantees. These poor people spend their lives in terror of accidentally damaging something.

Even if they make it to the end of their life without damaging anything, which is im-possible, since the human body attacks and kills germs and microbes *by the millions* every day with its immune system, that can only guarantee that current lifetime. There is still karma from earlier lifetimes to deal with.

It would be like spending money on a credit card every month for years and being borrowed up to the maximum, then finally getting to a month where you didn't spend a cent on credit! It would be good, but you'd still have the hundreds of months' past debt to pay off.

I never knew a witch who came **close** to living the kind of "harmless" life it would take to improve. Yet if those witches don't live like the Jains, they will keep digging themselves a deeper hole of bad karma from life to life **(they think!)**. Honestly, friends, can this really be done? If you're really thinking this through, you'll admit it cannot!

The Problem of Memory and Discipline

This won't take nearly as long to deal with, although it also entails a logical absurdity. A central question which the Reincarnationist must answer is, *"if we all lived before, why do we not remember our prior lives?"* There are various mystical answers to this, but they all boil down to the doctrine that going through the death/rebirth process wipes out our memories of past lives. Some call this "The Veil of Forgetfulness."

It is only through occult mediumship or meditation (both demanding practices which can take years to achieve) that one can supposedly learn about one's past lives. In my personal case, I had a prominent medium (or channeller) tell me a couple of my past lives, which she allegedly discerned through reading the akashic records.[1]

However, it must be granted by even the most diligent students of Reincarnation that the vast majority of people live and die without knowing or caring whether they had previous lives. As a result, most people stumble through their life with no idea what they are supposed to be learning or "paying back."

Is this sensible or logical? How can we learn if we are never told our mistakes? It is like taking a test and never learning our grade, yet being expected to do better the next time around.

A more mundane example shows the fallacy here. Suppose you have a dog that makes a mess on the living room rug. You let good old Fido go his merry way for a couple of weeks, then one day you smack him smartly on the nose with a rolled up newspaper and say "BAD DOG!"

Will Fido know the crime for which he is being punished? Of course not. He will be bewildered and utterly mystified as to why his master is chastising him. The simplest book on dog obedience makes it clear that you must immediately confront and firmly punish a dog for his offense. Yet we are asked to believe that the awesome universal force of karma doesn't have the good sense of a dog trainer.

The human being "punished" by misfortune for a past life he doesn't remember is just as bewildered or mystified as Fido. Unless he happens to be one of the select few who are educated or wealthy enough to study up on karma and past life regression or go to a medium for a reading, he will go through his entire life in this moral stupor, utterly unable to make sense of the cruel blows life seems to be dealing him.

Often, Christians and other non-believers in Reincarnation are accused of being "de-evolutionary" because we foster ignorance of the doctrine. Many psychics have taught that ignorance of Reincarnation is de-evolutionary and is a hindrance to spiritual growth. But this raises another paradox.

If it is contrary to the cosmic laws of growth to be ignorant of Reincarnation, why does the cosmos (or whatever) make the person forget about Reincarnation when they are born? This makes no sense at all. It is as if the "gods" or whatever are playing cruel tricks on man. They are deliberately withholding from him the very knowledge he needs most to mature.

He has no way of knowing what, if anything, he needs to do to make the pain and punishment stop! Is this justice? Is this good disciplinary practice? Sadly, the answer is no. If parents treated their child in this fashion, we would call them fiendish or at best, stupid. Yet we are asked to believe that this is the way the universe works. It is nonsense!

The Problem of Fatalism

As cruel as the last dilemma appears, this one is even more demanding. The logical end of karma is the ultimate version of the *Que sera, sera!* attitude — whatever will be will be.

There is a striking scene in leading Reincarnationist/New Age spokesperson Shirley MacLaine's book and miniseries, *Out on a Limb*. In the Andes mountains, Shirley and her "guru" or mentor in New Age paganism encountered an accident in which a busload of school children have gone over a steep cliff and been smashed to bits on the rocks below.

Shirley, naturally, expresses dismay at this tragedy and her guru gently chides her for her unevolved attitude. All those children wanted to die, needed to die, he explains. They all had "higher selves" which knew best — that it was good for their karma to be smashed to pieces at such a tender age. Besides, he smiles, there really is no death, only **transitions.** Thus whatever happens to people is intended to happen to them either by the blind machinery of karma or their own "higher self" or "god self."

This has led to some of the most wretched conditions in the world in the nation which has had the longest commitment to Reincarnation, India. If you see a beggar wallowing in the gutter in Calcutta, don't you dare help him! He is working out karma. If you take him in and give him a hot meal, new clothes and a good job;

he will just have to come back in another lifetime and be a beggar all over again. It is better that he get it over with!

This is why the idea of charity or kindness is so foreign to India, and why there were no hospitals or charitable institutions there until the advent of Christianity and the coming of Christian missionaries.

Might this be why there are no witch hospitals or orphanages? Because at the heart of their Reincarnationist beliefs is the idea of fatalism. That whatever is, is — and there is not a thing you can or should do about it!

This all sounds bad enough in the abstract, but let's apply this monstrous doctrine to our own lives. Suppose Mr. Witch comes home after a hard day at the organic farm and finds his dear wife, Mrs. Witch, being raped by a hoodlum. If he stops the attack, he is interfering with his wife's higher self. She has decreed for herself that this day she will be humiliated and abused. If her husband beats the crook off, she will just have to go through it again. *Plus* she will have incurred the further negative karma of having injured the poor rapist, who was, after all, only obeying both her higher self and his higher self, since higher selves always move in concord.

Hitler might have been brought into being by the higher selves of all those Jews! Perhaps we messed up the karma of Europe by interfering. Perhaps Jim Jones might have been caused by the 900 some people he drove to suicide down in the jungles of Guyana.

The logical end of the doctrine of karma is that one should never interfere in anything — never do anything. In the eastern countries from which this doctrine springs, the holiest men are those who *literally do nothing* — the gurus and siddhis who sit in "lotus" pose for weeks in their own filth and watch the weeds grow up around their legs!

Is this really a sane belief? I think not!

By this time, our friends who are sincere witches and believers in Reincarnation may be saying: *"That might be true of India and their approach, but that is not what I believe!"* That might be true, but does it change the reality?

Isn't this an essential part of the whole Reincarnationist process? Aren't the unmanageable mountains of bad karma and the fatalism all integral parts of the whole concept? How can you honestly have Reincarnation without them? You may not believe in this kind of severity and fatalism, but are you being internally consistent and honest with yourself if you deny these elements?

Aren't you just picking the parts of it that appeal to you and discarding the parts that challenge or offend you, or seem impossible to you? Can you do that and be true to both logic and history? I tried, my friend, and I finally had to admit that the whole system is an organic whole. It would be like saying, "I want a human body, but leave off the armpits because I don't like them."

You'd have a pretty silly body without armpits, and you'd have torn out the very warp and woof of Reincarnation by denying the doctrines of Ahimsa and fatalism. You're stuck with them, unless you want to try something better!

Empirical Testing

Finally, we have the problem of whether this belief has any concrete physical proof. If we are going to hold such a strange and illogical doctrine, we had better have some solid, empirical proof for it.

This proof could come in two forms: 1) actual testimonies of people who remember past lives and can validate those memories; and 2) anthropological evidence that the world is indeed "evolving."

There are books full of supposed testimonies of people who claim to have remembered past lives. Some of these accounts are quite extraordinary. Perhaps the classic work in this field, TWENTY CASES SUGGESTIVE OF REIN-CARNATION[2] has several such case studies of people who have apparent memories of existences in previous lifetimes in locales foreign to their current environment. These memories are often amazingly accurate and there does not seem to be any way in which the

153

person could have acquired the information which they possess except by having actually lived the past life.

However, a true scientific and empirical experiment must eliminate all other variables except the control. Even the quite scholarly author of the above mentioned book admits that he has not been able to do this. There is one other place these persons could have acquired this information — from *demon spirits* who have existed for thousands of years. He admits that this is a viable alternative theory to explain these memories.[3]

In true scientific method, if such a variable cannot be tested for, controlled or otherwise ruled out, then the experimental data is totally invalid. This is just common sense! Therefore, these memories, however impressive, cannot be considered empirical proof of Reincarnation. Since the possibility of demonic input of memories cannot be eliminated conclusively, we shall have to look elsewhere for evidence.

As far as looking at the world-wide anthropological data, there is even less support for Reincarnation as a viable hypothesis. There are a couple of serious problems here. First is the fact that the world population is growing at a geometric pace. If we are all being recycled, where are all the new babies coming from?

Say there were around 100 million people in the world in the time of Christ. Today there are five billion! That is fifty times more people. How did the fifty people today emerge from the one corresponding soul of a couple of millennia ago?

There are two answers to this which the Reincarnationists give, but both do some violence to the system of belief. Some say that the "gods" or the cosmos or whatever, is constantly creating new spirits. However, that does not set too well with the generally pantheistic worldview of witchcraft or Paganism. If there is no transcendent God "out there" apart from us, who is doing the creating of new souls?

In other words, pantheism is, by definition, a closed system. There can be no God "outside" of it, or it would be theism and take a giant step toward Biblical belief. Pantheism presupposes a cyclical birth-death-rebirth circle, which cannot be broken into by an outside force.

The other theory to explain population growth moves into science fiction's domain by proposing that the rebirth "pool" is interplanetary or even interstellar! As our planet grows in population, souls from Venus or Mars planet-hop over to us as those worlds die out and ours flourishes. This makes a certain strange kind of sense, if it weren't for the more serious anthropological argument against Reincarnation, which we will now look at.

If Reincarnation was true, and we all are evolving gradually through many lifetimes, then the logical thing to look for would be a demonstrable improvement in human nature over the centuries. Are we seeing this?

Humanists were very hopeful about this around the turn of the century. Progress in science and technology was pressing forward and war seemed about to be eliminated. However, the past eighty years have been an ugly reminder of how nasty (dare I say *sinful*) human beings are.

We have had two world wars of unparalleled human destruction; the genocide of Hitler and Stalin; and the organized enslavement of billions of people under communism in a fashion which would put the Roman emperors to shame. A case could be made for this being one of the worst centuries in recorded history. If we are so "evolved" why are we fighting wars with ever more dreadful weapons of destruction? Why has this century produced people like Adolph Hitler and Charles Manson (both devout believers in Reincarnation)?

Actually, war in the Middle Ages was more "civilized." There were certain days upon which you couldn't fight; and there were certain people who were protected (non-combatants). Today, with terrorism, babies and women are blown up wholesale. All we have done is become more indiscriminate and efficient in our war.

Can anyone say that our cities are more "evolved" today than they were fifty years ago? Of course not! The sad truth is that there is *no* evidence that we are perfecting in anyway, except perhaps in the technological arena.

Even there, SIN enters the arena. We split the atom and promptly use it to blow up two Japanese cities. We create amazing computers and before long, "viruses" and "tapeworms" are showing up in software maliciously destroying data and productivity. We have amazing medical breakthroughs, and more people are sick today than ever! We have immensely productive farms and yet people all over the world are starving by the millions.

If this is Reincarnation's salvation, it is a particularly lamentable effort.

We have mentioned the country which is the cradle of Reincarnation, India. Surely, with all the gurus and holy men, and the hallowed traditions of thousands of years of effort to achieve *ahimsa,* India should be the most evolved country on earth. Empirically, it should be a veritable textbook case of human progress and spirituality.

Anyone with even a passing acquaintance with India's history and current condition knows that such is the ***farthest thing from reality!*** India is probably one of the world's most woeful nations. Though it has almost as much fertile land as America, large portions of its people starve and live in utter poverty. Its caste system (rooted in Reincarnation) has led to centuries of bloodshed and bigotry.

The prime minister of India was cut down in a *religious* war between two rival Reincarnationist sects! India is said to be building thermonuclear weapons. Its city streets are awash with human and cattle waste, and lined with starving beggars! Cows and rats eat their fill while humans starve because these animals are considered sacred in Hindu theology! If India were an advertisement for Reincarnation, it wouldn't earn many converts.

So, we must ask, where is the empirical proof for Reincarnation? There appears to be precious little, either in the world at large, or in its most solid doctrinal citadel, India.

What Does the Bible Say?

Having looked at Reincarnation from a secular, logical point of view and found it wanting; let us now look at what another source of information has to say, God's Word, the Bible.

In my pilgrimage through the various forms of paganism, I finally came to the conclusion that I needed something solid to trust in. Although I had been told by my teachers in the occult all sorts of things about the Bible, when I checked them out for myself, I found that they were not telling me the truth.

I found that the Bible has a ***much better*** track record than any of the occult or mystical authors in whom I had put my trust. A thorough defense of the Bible is beyond the scope of this book, but suffice it to say that in my case, after reading literally *hundreds* of books on witchcraft, magic and esoteric philosophy; I finally found that only the Bible had real, ***solid*** answers to my questions! Every other author's work seemed to dissolve into a bland, metaphysical nonsense compared with the Bible.

So what does this Bible offer as its opinion on Reincarnation? And what concept of the afterlife does it actually teach?

First, the Bible clearly teaches that we have but **one** life in which to live. Hebrews 9:27 says:

> It is appointed unto men **once** to die, but after this the judgement.

Jesus Christ, Who is often mentioned by witches and New Agers as a man with many past lives in which He prepared Himself for His important work is actually said in Bible teaching to have incarnated only once (Hebrews 9:25-28). Not only that, but Jesus will never have to die again! (Romans 6:9)

Also, the key concept behind Reincarnation, that we can somehow perfect ourselves through our own effort, is vigorously denied by the Bible. The Bible teaches that:

> For by grace are ye saved through faith, and that ***not of yourselves***, it is the ***gift*** of God: Not of works, lest any man should boast.   Ephesians 2:8-9

Elsewhere, the same inspired writer, Paul, says:

> By the deeds of the law there shall be no
> flesh [no person] justified...
>
> Romans 3:20

Deeds of the law are basically good deeds, works
which would be considered "good karma" in the
Reincarnationist view. Nor is this the view of
just the New Testament. Even in the Hebrew
scriptures, or Old Testament, we are taught by
the prophet Isaiah that:

> ...we are all as an unclean thing, and **all
> our righteousnesses are as filthy
> rags;** and we all do fade as a leaf; and
> our iniquities, like the wind, have taken
> us away. Isaiah 64:6

Note another important factor here, though.
The above passage from Ephesians also teaches
that salvation is a "gift of God." Do you have to
pay for a gift? Of course not! This tells us that
God's gift of eternal life is free of charge; we do
not have to earn it. Romans 6:23 says:

> The wages of sin is death, but the **gift** of
> God is **eternal life** through Jesus Christ
> our Lord.

Doesn't that sound a lot easier than spending
dozens of lifetimes on the not-so-merry-go-
round of karma, trying to keep from stepping on
a bug? Ironically, the very principle of *ahimsa*
which we have mentioned is quite similar to the
Old Testament Law in that it presents an almost

impossible system of rules to keep which basically ends up confronting people with their own inability to make it themselves. However, in the Law, at least, there was provision for mercy and cleansing before God. There is no such provision in the merciless engine of karma.

Since God is perfectly willing to give this gift of eternal life to anyone who asks Him for it in the name of His Son, Jesus Christ, it pretty well shoots down in flames the whole complicated works-system of karma and Reincarnation.

Can It Really Be True?

The question will doubtless come up, *"How can we determine if this is really the true answer? What makes this any more believable than Reincarnation?"* The fact that Jesus Christ, the source of our salvation, rose from the dead to demonstrate His power to save us.

You cannot believe in both the concepts of Resurrection and Reincarnation at the same time, although some New Age groups try.[4] The Christian doctrine of the Resurrection teaches that because of Jesus' bodily Resurrection from the grave, all the dead will one day rise from the dead with "resurrection bodies." Those made righteous by Jesus' sacrifice on the cross will rise with glorified bodies of incredible beauty and power.

Those who reject Jesus will have to wait about a thousand years and then will rise in resurrected bodies which will not be any picnic to live in, especially since those bodies will be eternally confined to the lake of fire.

If you keep being reborn in different bodies, how are you going to shoehorn a resurrection in there? And if you did, which of the *hundreds* of bodies would you be resurrected in? Would you be a man or a woman?

Most witches and other Pagans have been led to believe that the resurrection of Jesus is just a myth. This is what I was taught as a witch. Some witches say that Jesus did rise, but it was just another version of the ancient Pagan "slain and risen god" archtype, like Osiris or Attis.

The problem with that concept is that Jesus is more than a myth, and His resurrection is much more than a myth! It is testified to directly by at least three eyewitnesses in the New Testament; John, Matthew and Peter, all of whom testified to seeing the risen Lord! On top of that, over 500 people saw Jesus after His resurrection, including the other eight apostles, Mary Magdalene and the disciples on the road to Emmaus! (1 Corinthians 15:6).

That is quite a lot of witnesses! It is more than enough to convict someone of murder! If you had a trial and four eyewitnesses testified to seeing you murder someone, plus over 500 second-hand accounts, you'd be on death row! Please understand that there is no such evidence to support the supposed resurrection of Osiris. These various "god" stories happened in a mythic setting. Jesus' life, death and resurrection happened in a real place and time. His tomb is empty today! You can go see it!

The tombs of the great exponents of Reincarnation are filled with rottenness and bones — Gautama or Bodhiharma — all are dust. But Jesus is <u>still alive</u> today! There is a tremendous body of evidence to prove the reality of His Resurrection, and it would be beyond the scope of this book to get further into that issue.[5]

The bottom line is that there is valid, physical evidence to believe in what Jesus has to offer you; whereas all these mystical systems can offer to you is metaphysical twaddle.

Besides, isn't the prospect of living in resurrected glory with Jesus more appealing than spending a few more hundred lifetimes running around the wheel of karma like a gerbil? He makes it so easy for you. All you have to do is lay aside your pride and belief in all those Pagan gods and admit that they cannot save you. Ask Jesus to forgive your sins and save you from hell and be the Lord of your life. (Romans 10:9-13)

He is real, and will be delighted to meet you right where you are!

9

Power in the Blood

Sooner or later in the discussion of Witchcraft, the subject of "Blood rituals" or sacrifice comes up. Especially in the last few years, the issue of human sacrifice has also become a question of deep concern. No reasonable person can deny that ritual abuse and murder of both children and adults is taking place in this nation. The only controversy revolves around numbers involved, and whether there is an organized, nationwide network of cult killings, or are they simply isolated cases of insane people?

The part of this exchange which concerns us here is whether or not Witches use blood sacrifice, or animal/human sacrifice. The public position of Wiccan defenders has been that Witches are life-affirming people by their creed and they do not do blood sacrifice, especially the sacrifice of living things.

Once again, there is reason to doubt the truth of these assertions. Earlier in this book, the use of ritual bloodletting among many traditions of Wicca was well-documented; as well as the boasting by Wiccan authorities of incidents of sacrifice through whipping of Witches during the times of the Spanish Armada and the Battle of Britain.

That bloodletting was not severe, but it was also not an isolated occurrence. Additionally, it must be admitted that there is a great difference morally between a Witch giving her life willingly in a magical rite for some lofty goal and an unwilling victim. The former might well be a martyr!

However, these instances should establish that there is a belief in the magical efficacy of shedding blood in Witchcraft. The question is, to what degree is that efficacy exploited?

The Trail of Blood

Any student of the history of occultism and magic will find the use of blood to be a common thread which runs through virtually every magical text. All Witches are not magicians, but a large majority of them do study the classical texts and practice some sort of magic.

These books or *grimoires,* which are centuries old, are full of rituals involving putting blood on talismans, slitting the throats of animals and using their shed blood as a barrier or using blood in your incense or your potions. The magical use of blood to invoke or appease the dead or call down power dates back to well before the time of Christ.[1] Frequently, classic magic rites involve the digging up and/or dismemberment of human bodies.[2]

Sometimes talismans are traced in the practitioner's own blood![3] This is not unusual material! In fact, one of the most popular "how to" books of the 1970's Wiccan revival, MASTERING WITCHCRAFT, has rituals involving minor bloodletting for talismans of protection.[4]

How "true" is this bloodshed to the historical roots of Paganism? As has been shown in previous chapters, there is a ghastly trail of blood leading all the way up to today from virtually all these "gentle" Pagan cultures.

It would be difficult to find a Pagan culture which did not have some sort of animal or human sacrifice; or at least gory, ritual bloodletting. From African shamanistic cultures which practice everything from cannibalism to human sacrifice, to New World Pre-Columbian cultures like the Aztecs, whose altars of sacrifice are still stained with the blood of virgins and warriors, and whose wells are full of the bones of victims.

Even the Celts, fountainheads of Wicca, had their "Wicker Men" where both animals and people were offered as sacrifices on the Celtic holidays such as Samhain (Halloween). Both occult writers and Wiccan writers admit this.[5]

In our chapter on the goddess, we have documented human sacrifice in the Pagan temples of both Greece and Rome as well as the Indian subcontinent.

Many of the rituals of the Indians are ghastly. American Indian rites of passage are incredibly grisly, such as the "Sun Dance" of the Plains Indians. To this day, some of these ceremonies are performed on reservations.

Speaking of the present, we must mention the Pagan/magical religions of the New World which are done by Haitian, Cuban or Brazilian Witchcraft Priests. Voodoo, Santeria and Macumba rituals all involve copious animal sacrifices and even human sacrifices, as the recent horror in Matamoros revealed. Certain Voodoo rites, especially the Rada varieties, require the sacrifice of a *cabrit sans cornu,* the "Hornless Goat," code for a human being!

These are *not* just quaint ethnic religions, they are dangerous forms of fullblown Paganism which are threatening the Hispanic areas of some cities. Our Wiccan friends will say that these are not Witches, but again: does saying it make it so? We need to ask that question in light of *The Book of Shadows.* In the initiations contained therein we see that there are eight "Working Tools" of the Wicca.

Of these, two deserve our attention, the Black Handled Knife or "Athame" and the White-Handled Knife or "Boleen." The question might be asked, *"why have two knives which are identical except for the handle-color?"*

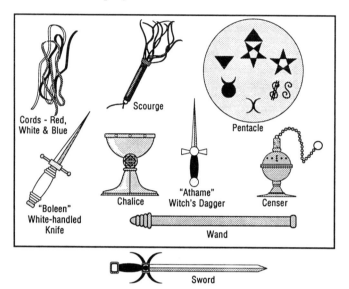

Cords - Red, White & Blue

Scourge

Pentacle

"Boleen" White-handled Knife

Chalice

"Athame" Witch's Dagger

Censer

Wand

Sword

The Working Tools of the Wicca

The answer given in the ritual is that the Athame is used as an instrument of magic only. It is "the true Witch's weapon and...has all the powers of the Magic Sword."[6] Those powers include being able to "form all Magic Circles, Subdue and punish all rebellious Spirits and Demons and even persuade the evil Genii. With this in your hand, Thou art ruler of the Magic Circle."[7]

The White-handled Knife has a different purpose. It is "to form all instruments used in the Art. It can only be used in a Magic Circle."[8] Now, what is communicated in the oral tradition

168

is that part of the reason for the distinction between knives is that the Athame must **never** be touched with blood, but the White-Handled knife is what is to be used to draw blood for ritual purposes.[9]

"Boleen"
White-handled
Knife

So we see that even in the "whitest" of "white" Witch groups, allowances are made in the eight working tools for a specialized tool to draw blood! I know that in our tradition, that knife was used many, many times.

The Divine King

We turn to the second of the two core myths of Witchcraft, the ritual of the Divine King, or Victim (the first being the Descent of the Goddess into the Underworld). This myth is better known, and has become a central feature of both anthropology and literature. Sources as divergent as the opera *Parsival* by Wagner, Sir James Frazer's THE GOLDEN BOUGH, and T.S. Eliot's monumental poem, *"The Waste Land,"* deal with the Divine King extensively.

Basically, the rite of Divine King teaches that the High Priest and/or King is magically linked to the land over which he ruled. If the High

Priest King (HPK) sickens, the land suffers. If he prospers, the land prospers. As Margaret Murray, a popular author among Wiccans, explains:

> There is a strong body of evidence to show that in the primitive cult of western Europe the god was sacrificed...The underlying meaning of the sacrifice of the divine victim is that the spirit of God takes up its abode in a human being, usually the king, who thereby becomes the giver of fertility to all his kingdom. When the divine man begins to show signs of age he is put to death, lest the spirit of God should also grow old and weaken like its human container...In some places the time of death was indicated by signs of approaching age, such as grey hair or loss of teeth; in other places a term of years was fixed, usually either seven or nine. When the changes inevitable to all human customs gradually took place, a substitute could suffer in the king's stead, dying at the time the king should have died and thus giving the king a further lease of life. This, put shortly is the theory and cult of the Dying God. The belief belongs to all parts of the Old World, and survives in Africa into the present century. It was a fundamental dogma of the pre-Christian religion of Europe...[10]

The Arthurian legend[11] deals with the Divine King or "Fisher King" as he is sometimes known.

He is the wounded king who can only be healed by contact with the Grail. In Christian versions of this legend, the Grail is said to be the cup Jesus used at the Last Supper; but in older Pagan versions, it is the cauldron of the goddess or a metaphor for sex with the goddess. A "worthy" knight of the Round Table (often Sir Parsifal) delivers the Grail to the king and heals him and thus restores the fertility of the land.[12]

Like most Pagan myths, this one has a dark side. There comes a time when the HPK (High Priest King) can no longer rule, so he must be slain for the good of the land. His blood must spill out upon the land to restore its fertility.

Wicca honors this myth in its cycle of sabbats in which the god dies, and is reborn. A High Priest is only allowed to reign in traditional covens for seven years. Then he must retire and be replaced by a younger, virile Priest. This was to forestall him becoming impotent. If, however, the land of the covendom (his "kingdom") becomes infertile, then the High Priest was *slain* in an act of ritual sex with his High Priestess. He would have his throat slit with the Boleen at the *exact* moment of his climax with his High Priestess as Goddess, and his blood was believed to fertilize the soil.

He goes to his death willingly, so this is not so much ritual murder as it is ritual suicide. I was *fully* prepared (and indeed felt honored) for this if things grew bad under the years of my High Priesthood. Fortunately for me, they did not, and I lived to become a High Priest emeritus.

This ceremony is a reflection of countless myths of slain and risen gods[13] all the way back to the slain Nimrod in Babylon. Nimrod's wife Semiramis (who was also his mother) asserted that her child by him was the new "Nimrod," and the old Nimrod, now dead, became a god.[14] This fraud religion began this myth, which is reflected to this very day in the Wiccan concept of the eternal Goddess (Semiramis) and her son/lover the Horned God (Nimrod and Nimrod, jr.) who dies and is reborn every year.

Three recent films, which have a following among Witches, that treat this ritual thoroughly and accurately are *Excalibur, The Wicker Man,* and the "mini-series" *Harvest Home.*

This ritual slaying of the HPK is so deeply enshrined in Witchcraft and Paganism that Dr. Margaret Murray, the woman most responsible for the Wiccan revival in this century and its patron scholar, spends an entire chapter of one of her books discussing how various kings of England (or their ritual substitutes) were thus ritually slain and how integral this ritual cycle of the Divine King is to Wicca.[15] With this kind of bloody ceremonial drama so profoundly intermingled with the legends and deities of Wicca, how can we avoid concluding that blood rituals are being done.

However, the same Dr. Murray whom the Wiccans use to prove their ancient history asserts that the Witch cult in medieval Europe did indeed practice child-sacrifice and cannibalism, however rarely.[16] It would seem to me that once would be too often. Wiccans are either performing blood rituals, or they are betraying the very historicity which they claim to cherish so highly.

Why all the Blood?

The question arises, why this emphasis on blood? An understanding of the magical/shamanistic world view clarifies this. With a couple of possible exceptions, there is no element within the human or animal body so associated with magic power, life and life energy than the blood.[17] Even the Bible says:

> For the life of the flesh is in the blood.
> Leviticus 17:11

To a Witch, to consume blood is to consume life. To shed blood is to release an incredible amount of "life energy." To shed enough blood to kill a person is to release *incalculable* amounts of magical power, enough perhaps to even keep a "god" alive. This belief among most Witches that their god needs their rituals to keep going is perhaps the most striking difference between Pagan theology and the Biblical God. As Sir James Frazer recounts:

> Man has created gods in his own likeness and being himself mortal, he has naturally supposed his creatures to be in

173

the same sad predicament. Thus, the Greenlanders believed that a wind could kill their most powerful god, and that he would certainly die if he touched a dog. When they heard of the Christian God, they kept asking if he never died, and being informed that he did not, they were much surprised, and said that he must be a very great god indeed...a North American Indian stated that the world was made by the Great Spirit. Being asked which Great Spirit he meant, the good one or the bad one, "Oh, neither of them," replied he, "the Great Spirit that made the world is dead long ago. He could not possibly have lived as long as this."[18]

This pathetic view of "the god" is common to almost all Pagan peoples, up to the present day. Virtually all Pagans have this defective view of God as a finite, limited being. We met occasionally with some covens from Chicago that seriously believed that if they didn't keep faithful in their performance of the eight main seasonal sabbats of Wicca, the sun would not "return from the south" and the entire cycle of seasons would grind to a cosmic halt and the earth would wither and die.

If your god is dependent upon frequent blood sacrifices to keep going, then this sort of theology explains the reasoning behind modern Wiccan theology. This magic world view of their gods is the justification for most blood rituals, including cannibalism and vampirism.

It is because of this Pagan belief that the Lord God forbade his people from eating blood in the very same chapter of the Bible just quoted above, because all the Pagan peoples around Israel were drinking blood, both animal and human; and the Lord wished them to steer as far as possible from such loathsome practices.

We need to ask, is it *reasonable* to believe that with centuries of blood sacrifice in the background of every Pagan culture, witches of the past century would suddenly have stopped? Although we certainly do not want to smear an entire sub-culture, it is the testimony of most Witches who "come out" of Wicca that blood rituals *are* going on.

Many of the Wiccans with whom we associated did blood rituals, including the Divine King and forms of ritual vampirism. I, myself, did many rituals in which I had to open either my veins or someone else's veins to provide blood.

"Blood Lust"

Are there deeper reasons for this strange pattern of blood letting in magic and Witchcraft? Can we go beyond the anthropological clichés and discover a more subtle trap awaiting us? The answer must be yes, for there are spiritual issues which strike at the very heart of the Pagan/Christian dichotomy.

Contrary to popular belief, the Lord is not this "spoilsport" in the sky who thunders down His

"Thou shalt nots" just to keep us from having fun. It is helpful to think of His Bible as an "Owner's Manual" for human beings.

My owner's manual for the computer I am using to write this book tells me not to dump soft drinks into my computer terminal. Does it tell me that to deprive me of the exquisite pleasure of pouring a Coke into a computer? Of course not! It gives that warning because it is the nature of electrical devices to not do well around randomly splashing liquids.

Similarly, we do not rail against our auto manufacturers for telling us to periodically change the oil in our cars. However, God is our "manufacturer" (as much as people today hate to admit it) and He knows more about how to keep people running smoothly than anyone else. That is all the commands in the Bible are: God's instructions for how to achieve happiness, full authentic personhood and deep spiritual fulfillment. We ignore those instructions at our peril.

We are not surprised if a computer shorts out after being deluged in soda; yet we are thunderstruck to learn that if people use each other sexually in ways that are contrary to the Manufacturer's instructions, they will biologically "short out" their immune systems.

This same principle can be applied to the Lord's commands against the Pagan use of blood-letting. It is instructive to note that even in the New Testament, the early church carried over only four things from the Law and laid them on the new Gentile (non-Jewish) Christians. They were to refrain from:

1. Eating meat offered to idols.
2. Eating blood.[19]
3. Eating animals that had been killed by strangling.
4. Fornication (sexual immorality).[20]

When our Maker says something *that strongly, that often,* we need to pay attention. God knew that all the Pagan people around His children were practicing blood sacrifice of some sort. We can assume that He wished His children to stay away from it for a very good reason.

As we have already seen, in spite of God's commands, the Israelites continually slid back into the Pagan practices of their neighbors. Over and over again, those practices ultimately led them to the inconceivable desire to burn their infants alive in the fires of Molech![21]

Even today, we talk in common parlance about "blood lust." It does seem that even in our "civilized" society, there is an unwholesome fascination with blood. Our youth are being exposed to a deluge of films designed to simulate every imaginable manner of horrible, gore-drenched death. The "fake" blood gushes in gallons in these films, and they are among the top video rentals.

We've all experienced the disturbing phenomenon of driving down the highway and having a bottleneck occur at the scene of an accident because cars full of morbid curiosity-seekers slow to an unnecessary crawl to try and catch a glimpse of some poor mangled victim or splashes of blood on the highway. We are attracted and repelled at the same time by bloodshed. The sight of a human being's *literal life* running out onto the asphalt is compelling in a way we don't really understand.

A Strange Addiction

As I moved deeper into Witchcraft, past the Third Grade level, I found my own fascination with horror films increase geometrically. What began as an intrigue with classic horror films which had no gore, hemorrhaged into a desire to see ever more grotesque displays of charnel house delights.

I had a night job and my wife worked days, so I often had afternoons to kill. I religiously visited the matinees of virtually every new horror film. But something happened to me at one of these matinees which pulled me up sharply and forced me to take a look at myself.

I was sitting in a matinee, with only about two other people in the theater. During one scene where some totally gruesome things were being done to a female character, I heard these nearly orgasmic moans coming from a middle-aged woman two rows in front of me. I felt the hair stand up on the back of my neck! I decided I'd better leave. I felt grateful to be back out in the afternoon sunshine of Milwaukee. The eerie cries of that unfortunate woman echoed in my ears as I walked back to my car. I realized that she had been overcome in some mystical transport of sadism, or "blood lust." I felt unclean, like a voyeur caught witnessing some profoundly private moment of unhallowed intimacy. I resolved, at that point, to not go to any more of those films alone.

Since Sharon, my wife, couldn't stand them, I knew that I was effectively "taking the pledge." I simply didn't want to end up as a weird solitary addict to splatter movies, spending all my spare time alone in dingy theaters moaning at screens.

As I later learned in my involvement in higher levels of magic, there can be a real addiction to blood and gore, both real and celluloid. I found that it was taking ever more grisly movies to give me the "kick" I needed. When I started participating in real blood rituals, I found the act compelling.

I realize now that there is a real addiction in operation here, similar to the downward spiral which has been noted in much of substance abuse. Blood may well be one of the ultimate substances to abuse! I believe this is why God forbade His people to become involved in it.

Where Does It Stop?

In the sixties, we all scoffed at the threats of

grumpy officials that marijuana could be addictive or dangerous. We laughed the people to scorn who told us that cocaine was addictive. Today, we know that marijuana is dangerous and that cocaine can be even more addictive than heroin! If the last decades have taught us anything, they *should* have taught us that we flaunt the rules of conventional morality (which are often reflections of God's Law in most cases) at our own dire peril.

Here is the problem: once you grant, as most Wiccans seem to, the need for occasional ritual bloodletting, who is to say where that blood-letting will stop? I know that in 1972 I would have said that it would be <u>unthinkable</u> for me to drink someone's blood or do an animal sacrifice, that Witches do *not* do such things. Yet six years later I had participated in animal sacrifices and become involved deeply in ritual vampirism. Mine is not the only story which could chart that tragic trajectory.

One you "grant" that blood has magical power and efficacy, you seem to be carried along on a subtle, but inexorable course toward ever more graphic ways of getting it. I can honestly tell you that when the Lord began to draw me out of the occult, I was just millimeters away, spiritually, from being ready to do murder for my "Old Gods."

When I had the Horned God *"drawn down"* into me at the sabbats,[22] I found my body consumed with great magical power. However, my mind was filled increasingly with ghastly images of mutilation and death, which made the films I had attended seem like Winnie-the-Pooh by comparison.

At first, these strange, magically wrought fantasies manifested in paintings I created, and in the writing, both poetry and prose I did. However, these seemed to me but *safety valves* providing release for forces which were rapidly reaching critical mass. Every time I participated in a sabbat, especially during the winter months, it was as if the reservoirs of violence were refilled. The power of the "god" within me seemed to be driving me inexorably toward a breaking point, where I was growing more and more inured to the idea of death and pain. Was he not the "Lord of Death"?

I thank **the true God** that through the prayers of a Christian, He brought me back from that abyss!

Researchers seem to agree that violence in films desensitizes the viewers. It is evident in our culture that real violence desensitizes those that do it. I put it to you that ritualized violence is no different. We see this in cases like the executed mass-killer, Ted Bundy, who was involved in occultism and witchcraft at the University of Washington, as well as being addicted to increasingly violent and perverse forms of pornography.

Bundy was not an isolated kook. He was a

charming, brilliant and personable young man, and was part of a larger group of occultists *still practicing to this day*. People like him, Charles Manson, "Night Stalker" Richard Ramirez and, to a lesser degree, myself, are testimony of the seductive power of blood rituals.

One of our finest Wiccan pupils was so dedicated to the Craft that he flew to England to personally study under Alex Sanders. When he came back a few weeks later, for unknown reasons, he had become very intrigued with blood rituals. He started cutting himself up and doing repeated ceremonies involving the killing of chickens. When he finally "ritually" starved a black cat to death we got disgusted and, after warning him repeatedly, disfellowshipped him from the coven.

Ironically, a couple of years later, I began to **walk down the same road.** No one can say where this kind of magic can take you! Why did our friend get into it more rapidly than I? That's like asking why some people become drunks overnight and others take years. The point is, it is <u>deadly spiritual danger</u>.

REAL Power in the Blood

Why is the Lord so against this kind of blood rituals, and why do Pagans and Witches down through the millennia keep getting involved in them. The answer is simple. Satan is a copycat, and he is the author of all false religion. He knows the Bible well, so he knows that "without shedding of blood is no remission [of sins]." (Hebrews 9:22) and that "it is the blood that maketh an atonement for the soul." (Leviticus 17:11).

He knows that since the Garden of Eden and the slaying of an animal by God Himself to cover the sins and nakedness of Adam and Eve[23], the only way for a person's sins to be forgiven is through the shedding of blood. Thus, he created religious cults like Ba'al worship, Egyptian religion, Molech worship, and Nimrod and Semiramis, which taught people that the "gods" could only be appeased or maintained in their power by blood — often the blood of humans and infants.

This was a horrible mockery by Satan of the sacrifices of the Law of Moses which required **unspotted** animal sacrifices.[24] In place of animals without blemish, Satan substituted babies, their tender years being supposed to guarantee innocence. If babies could not be found, then virgin children (symbolically innocent and unblemished) had to be sacrificed.

So we find all these cultures whose shamans or priests believe that the only way the gods can be appeased was through the shedding of human blood. In this fashion, Satan twisted the meaning of the Old Testament sacrifices until they were barely recognizable.

When Jesus Christ came and died on the cross to offer His blood for the sins of the world, **_all_** blood sacrifice, even the animal sacrifices of the

Jewish temple, became meaningless and unnecessary. Just a drop of His precious blood was (and is) enough to cleanse the entire world of its sin. There is no need for these sacrifices anymore, for they can never take away sin.[25]

However, because Satan fears the **power** of Jesus' blood so much, he keeps drawing people away from it by continuing animal and human sacrifices wherever he possibly can. This is why all the false religious cults emphasize the shedding of blood and mortification of the flesh, whether by sacrifice, whipping, wearing hair shirts or barbed wire corsets.

Even the Roman church exemplifies this obsession with blood in a classic Pagan fashion. It burned heretics and witches to appease God and many of its monastic orders and their followers practice whipping. Catholic fringe groups like *Los Penitentes* whip, torture and actually crucify people with the apparent blessing of the clergy during Lent and Holy Week, trying to "re-do" that which cannot and **should not** be repeated, the once-and-for-all sacrifice of Jesus on Calvary.

The central "Mystery" of the Roman church is the Mass, a daily sacrifice of Jesus anew on the altar, followed by the ritual drinking of His blood and eating His flesh. Devout Catholics believe that by doing these rites, they can appease God. Thus, they are tragically steered around the real sacrifice of the cross by Satan.

This Pagan "game" of blood is the same trick Satan uses the world over.

All Pagans keep desperately reaching for something that Satan is frantically trying to conceal from them; the power of the precious blood of the Lamb of God, Jesus Christ. This is because there is truly incredible power in His blood — not in ours, but in Jesus'.

I believe the use of blood in rituals so easily and so often disintegrates into acts of ritual violence and murder because it is such a clear violation of the commandments of God. Like any evil, it feeds upon itself and is never satisfied. The compulsions to perform these rituals grow stronger over the years, until finally you don't seem to have much control left at all, and the only thing that matters is the killing.

We may never know how many of these crazed killers whose work we so often see on the nightly news got their apprenticeship in Wicca, but I ask you, is it worth the risk? As we used to tell our initiates in *Alexandrian Wicca*, "You have placed your foot on the Path of the Lightning, and you may never leave it."

I left it, and I praise God that I did, but it was only **_His_** power and grace that kept me from becoming another Ted Bundy or Charles Manson. Ask Him for His help, in Jesus' name!

10

The Sacred Altar

In the last chapter we discussed one "downward spiral" which seems to happen to those that get involved in Wicca. Earlier, we looked at the Wicca and drugs. Here we are going to try to understand what Witches call "erecting the Sacred Altar" — the use and consequences of sexual magic. Thus, we have what might be called the "Unholy Triumvirate" of Witchcraft: sex, drugs and blood rites.

Sexuality is one battlefield where the lines should seem clearly drawn. Christians stand for monogamy and chastity! Oddly enough, many Wiccan authors used to go out of their way to try and make their religion sound reasonably monogamous and chaste as well. Alex Sanders, a leading spokesman for Wicca until his recent death, continually denied that any sort of unusual sex took place in his covens, aside from the nudity.[1]

This varies from group to group; and with the passage of time. By the mid-seventies, many

Wiccan leaders were adapting to the loosening climate of sexual mores by admitting that yes, "things" did happen at Witch meetings. Toward the end of that decade, things began to really open up; and homosexuals were being welcomed into covens and even entire rites of Wicca arose like the Order of Ganymede and the Dianic covens which were actually homosexual or lesbian in nature.

However, there remained an odd ambivalence about sexuality in the public statements concerning Witchcraft in those days. The "Great Rite," the Third Grade initiation was acknowledged to involve, more often than not, sexual intercourse; unless it was done "symbolically." Even then, many Witches insisted that the Great Rite was only done between husbands and wives or "perfect couples,"[2] and thus it could hardly be considered an orgy.

Other than that, most Witches insisted that their meetings were quite demure, and would satisfy the moral requirements of a Boy Scout troop leader, aside from the nudity.[3] All this demure talk is a bit strange coming from a religion which supposedly worships sex and human generation, as it is manifested in the male and female reproductive organs.

Wiccans are quite open about the fact that their wands are male symbols; and that their chalices are female symbols. Most of the Wiccan rites contained thinly veiled references to sex. When one considers how these same gods and goddesses used to be worshiped centuries ago, the supposed chastity of Wicca sounds a bit strained, to put it mildly.

No Consensus

As mentioned above, all Wiccan and Neo-Pagan groups are not quite as concerned with their public image in regard to chastity. Some are more willing to admit what goes on than others. *The Church of All Worlds,* while more Neo-Pagan than Wiccan, was one of the more "open" groups, and it made no bones about its endorsement of total sexual freedom. Some of the other more recent groups were also more frank about their interest in sex.

The Church of Wicca, mentioned in earlier chapters as controversial, literally "buried the meter" when it came to sex. The church's leaders, Gavin and Yvonne Frost, wrote a book, THE WITCH'S BIBLE: HOW TO PRACTICE THE OLDEST RELIGION. When it was released, it was greeted with howls of rage from many Witches who claimed that it was not Wiccan "orthodoxy."

Aside from its teaching that there was only one god who was sexually neuter, the main reason it blew the pentagrams off every Witch in town was that it talked publicly and in print about practices most Witches wished kept secret! Aside from revealing that group sex magic was practiced in covens, it also taught as normative

188

the defloration of girls surgically.[4] The ritual initiation into sex of pubescent boys and girls by older coven members[5] and the use of artificial "phalli" on the girl initiates to prepare them for sexual magic rites.[6]

Although these practices were common in many of the Wiccan groups I was involved with, along with a few other equally bizarre practices, the Frosts became the object of a firestorm of vituperation because they were tarnishing the carefully-wrought Wiccan public image. Just when folks like Sybil Leek had succeeded in toning down the "orgies on the hilltop" image of Wicca, along came the Frosts and wrecked the whole thing.

The bottom line is; the *Church of Wicca* was essentially cast out from most other Pagan and Neo-Pagan organizations, and yet remains, almost twenty years later as a barely acknowledged "black sheep" organization on the fringes of the Craft. Their only crime was insisting on authenticity and telling the truth. Hell hath no fury like a Witch exposed!

Sex Magic

The sex magic techniques which the Frosts dared to describe were nothing new.[7] The use of group sex without climax in the Magic Circle for raising power had already been revealed in the occult literature; but in the context of Eastern religion or Tantra Yoga, which is the magical practice of having sex with your "god" or "goddess" (i.e. demons). More recently, it has been openly discussed by "orthodox" Wiccan authors like Doreen Valiente, who gives a brief but thorough treatise on Tantra in one of her books.[8]

Almost all Wiccan groups believe that the Magic Circle exists as a kind of spiritual pressure cooker designed to hold occult energy in a "cone of power" until it had built to the point of release. At the point the High Priestess discerns that it has arrived at "critical mass," it is, so to speak, aimed and fired at the intended target, like a mystic cruise missile, although often with benign intent (we are told).

Desire is held to be one of the keys to building this etheric energy cone. In simple terms, if you *really* want that job, your desire will make the cone of power that more efficacious in getting you the job. Once you get past the First Grade in Wicca, you are taught that one of the most easily invoked and powerful forms of desire is sexual desire.

However, if that desire is "earthed" by climax, then the cone of power is depleted. Thus, the form of sexual magic the Frosts and many traditional covens teach involves maintaining high levels of sexual arousal for as long as possible without release. This is believed to be one of the most powerful forms of "Right Hand" Tantra or sexual "white" magic, called *maithuna*. To prevent everyone from becoming frustrated, in the period following the release of the cone of power, there is a time of "relaxation" when everyone can cut loose.

"Right hand" Tantra Yoga is felt to be noble and related to the solar energies of the god. However, in spite of their goddess-worship, most Wiccans claim to steer clear of "Left Hand" or *Vama Marg* Tantra,[9] which is <u>lunar</u> and related to the goddess. However, when you are worshiping a goddess it is difficult to ignore her impulses. Thus, many Witches find themselves getting involved in more and more unusual forms of sexual activity.

"Left hand" Tantra involves perverse heterosexual activity, to begin with; as well as ritual bondage and flagellation,[10] as has been previously described in the Wiccan initiation rites. It then proceeds downward into homosexuality, sado-masochistic practices and beyond. I honestly don't know too many Wiccans who were able to stay out of the "Left hand" Tantric material once they entered the High Priesthood.

Our culture has come to regard many of these practices as off-center but basically alright. This is not what the Word of God says though, and the sins of sexual perversion are among those most severely condemned after practices like murder and child sacrifice. Contrary to the "liberal" line in some churches, God does not smile upon homosexuality or sadism! He condemns the sin, but loves the sinner and calls him or her to repentance.

Mr. Crowley Again

We have already documented the pervasive influence of Aleister Crowley upon the beginnings of Wicca; and Gerald Gardner's masochistic tendencies which he managed to work into his Wiccan rituals. Crowley did a great deal to reveal the secrets of Tantra to the occult student. As has been mentioned, most Witches, myself included, find it necessary to study his material and "plug themselves into" the magical current of Crowley's demon spirit guide, a mysterious being named *Aiwass.*

Aiwass is another name for Set,[11] an Egyptian god mentioned earlier. He is a central deity to Wiccans, whether they wish to acknowledge it or not; for his sigil or symbol is the star or pentagram, especially inverted,[12] which is the sign of Second Grade in the *Alexandrian Wicca.*

Probably no symbol is more commonly associated with Wicca than the pentagram. It is on the first page of the *Book of Shadows,* and is even prominently displayed on the pamphlet put out by Laurie Cabot's Witches' League for Public Awareness. Thus it may be seen that one of the most central symbols of the Wicca is a talisman to invoke the god, Set or Aiwass. He is certainly one of the oldest forms of the "god" of the Wicca.[13] No matter how hard our "white" Witch friends try, they cannot avoid tripping over Mr. Crowley and his methods.

Crowley exemplified both Right and Left-hand

paths of Tantra. He was a sadist and a promiscuous bisexual. He was deeply involved with hard-core drugs, including heroin, cocaine, morphine and opium. In short, he was everything Witches try to pretend they are not.

Without going into more gory details than necessary, the sexual magic Crowley brought to the West from his travels in Egypt, Nepal, Tibet and Ceylon involved the belief that various orifices of the body were tunnels into other magical dimensions — alternate realities or "anti-matter universes;" and that sexual fluids were magical elixirs if properly "consecrated" by a Priestess of the Art in a Magic Circle.

In bringing these secrets out in his privately published books, Crowley skated the edge of revealing the very highest secrets of both Templary and Freemasonry. Those who followed his teaching, which included members of the English-speaking branches of the O.T.O., and a large majority of the Third Grade and beyond Witches I knew, rapidly became obsessed with sadism, sodomy, perversion and both physical and psychic vampirism!

The Trap of "The Beast"

Crowley styled himself "The Great Beast" after the anti-Christ in Revelation 13. His full name, Edward Alexander Crowley, added up to 666 in Hebrew and Greek qabalahs. One of the magical titles he took was TO MEGA THERION, which was Greek for "The Great Beast."

Although Crowley publicly disdained Witchcraft, he managed to exert an overwhelming influence upon its early development in this century. Through his relationship with Wiccan leaders like Gardner, Sybil Leek and Alex Sanders, Crowley seems to have had the last diabolical laugh. He managed to fill the mystic geography of Wicca with a plethora of psychic land mines of deadly intensity. No matter where the Wiccan student places her foot, her magic is likely to explode in highly unexpected ways.

The Book of Shadows' highest level rituals have whole passages quoted verbatim out of Aiwass' demonic dictation, *Liber AL vel Legis,* or *The Book of the Law,* the "Bible" of Crowley's New Age religion, Thelema.[14] The very core of the Wiccan law, the *Wiccan Rede,* reads like a pale pastiche of Crowley's command, "Do what thou wilt shall be the whole of the law."[15] The pentagrams, inverted and upright, which are invoked at every Wiccan circle are the signs to invoke the perverse and demonic god, Set.

The central deity of Wicca, the Goddess, is borrowed, right down to ritual paraphernalia, from the first chapter of *The Book of the Law*. No matter where the serious magical Wiccan apprentice turns, he or she is confronted with Crowley's magical "current" of energy. When a High Priest or High Priestess is created in ritual initiation, they are usually empowered by an act of Tantric sex, while invoking a powerful ritual written by Crowley himself for his blasphemous and satanic "Gnostic Mass".[16]

194

True, traditional Witchcraft teaches that for a High Priest or Priestess of the Third Grade to be made, sexual contact must be made in a sexual magic environment (Third Grade circle) between the Priestess' cervix and the Priest's organ. This supposedly closes a magical link, much like an electrical circuit between the two neural physiologies of the man and woman involved.

It is only through this closed circuit that supposedly the super-essential wisdom and power of the High Priesthood can be passed between Initiator and Candidate. This is why the "symbolic" Great Rite so often spoken of, in which the invocation is followed by dipping an athame into a chalice, is actually a magical sham.

This is what the Third Grade Invocation actually means when it says:

> Open for me the secret way: the pathway of Intelligence between the gates of night and day, beyond the boundaries of time and sense. Behold the Mystery aright. The Five Points of Fellowship, here where Lance and Grail unite, and feet and knees and breasts and lips.[17]

It is in this utterly intimate contact that the "power" of the High Priesthood is passed, and has been passed down through the generations. Crowley designed this ritual to continue the highly depraved Set (or Aiwass) magical current from the Initiator to the candidate.[18] At the risk of stretching a metaphor, he created a *spiritual venereal disease,* which could be easily passed through the act of sex, and which would insure that his "religion" would survive long after his death.

In this fashion, Crowley has managed to place his mark on every Wiccan leader for several generations. He has introduced a strain of *demonic virus* into the very beating spiritual heart of the Wicca and created an apostolic succession of unparalleled debauchery and evil.

Every time a Witch, of whatever tradition, casts a pentagram; she is invoking Crowley's demonic god, Set. Without realizing it, she has set off a spiritual tripwire trap set a half-century ago! She has brought forth within herself the spirit of the Aeon of the Crowned and Conquering Child which Crowley hoped to produce, and she is standing on extremely perilous footing.

Certainly, there are Wiccan traditions which do not use any material either from Gardner or Crowley. However, in my experience, they are in the distinct minority. I knew many Witches who began as Gardnerian or Alex-andrian and then branched off to start their own "Traditions." If any of these people had received the High Priesthood in the manner described, they would be sexual "carriers" of the Aiwass current, whether they knew it or not.

Since most Witches are not monogamous, and

since they gather frequently at regional and national Pagan festivals, you can bet that this evil sexual current has been spread (almost like AIDS) between the entire Pagan and Neo-Pagan community!

So unless a Witch has totally avoided sex with other Witches, and has never used pentagrams or other Setian current imagery, she is probably already caught in the jaws of the Great Beast's trap.

Crowley left behind him a tragic parade of insane women and suicidal men as his disciples. Is it any wonder that today Witches, either male or female, who unknowingly invoke his power and use his rituals, often end in very dire straits emotionally and spiritually?

Perhaps the occasional Witch will say, "I don't get into Crowley and I never mess with his rituals. I don't use the Gardnerian *Book of Shadows.*" That may be, but Crowley's influence is in places where you least expect it, and it will rear up like a serpent and strike you when you are least able to prepare for it.

A Blueprint for Depravity

In so many cases of friends of mine from the Craft, I watched this current do its awful work. I have already mentioned the descent into blood rites, but additionally sexual perversity of the vilest sort enthralled many of them. I was not immune either.

197

Like a beetle which eats invisibly away at a piece of wood, the demonic powers unleashed by Wiccan initiations gnawed silently at whatever decency and sanity we possessed. Many of us became involved in sado-masochism and bondage and discipline. Hard-core pornography, promiscuity and adultery were taken for granted.

Sodomy is especially "sacred" to Set because of its close association to human waste, and its mimicry of certain canine practices.[19] This detestable practice serves a similar function in the anus as does the magical sex act of intercourse described above. It opens what are called the "Typhonion"[20] tunnels, channels through which extremely powerful demons, like the horrible Choronzon,[21] can travel from their "alternate reality" and emerge into this universe and enter the sex partner's body.

This is what is called *Qliphotic* magic, representing the **blackest** side of Qabalism and the Tree of Life. The *Qliphot* (derived from the Hebrew for "harlot"[22] or "shell") is the "backside" of the qabalistic Tree of Life.[23] The "backside" metaphor carries through, for the best way to open these tunnels of demonic ingress is through homosexual sex, in which approximate contact and stimulation is achieved with the prostate gland of the other.

As study of occult anatomical principles reveals that it is believed that a circuit of powerful energy runs from the anus to the roof of the mouth and tongue, down through the trunk and into the generative organs.[24] Thus, it can be seen that most homosexual practices reinforce these demonic links. This does much to explain both the increasingly perverse and even dangerous practices of most homosexuals, and of most people who practice higher levels of Witchcraft.

This also explains the sudden meteoric rise of interest in the child as a sexual object, and the *terrible* seductiveness of child pornography. We often ask ourselves, "How could a person be sexually attracted to a small child?" It does not seem sane or normal, and of course it is not. Yet, throughout his life, Crowley attempted to invoke the Crowned and Conquering Child.

A key element within the Aiwass current and the Left-hand path is that of the beguiling or fascinating child.[25] Crowley's magical current was designed to compel an interest in ever younger and younger sexual partners as a way of "reifying" alchemically, or bringing into manifestation the worship of the child-god, Heru-Paar-Kraat!

Add to this the sexually vampiric belief that the younger the person you abuse, the more power or vitality you can extract from them, and you have a potent recipe which explains the obsession with children. Witches who practice this kind of sexual Tantra believe they are both emotionally and literally stealing the youth of the child they are abusing.

199

The legacy of the Set/Aiwass current which so permeates modern Wicca is thus a blueprint for depravity! My first ritual homosexual experience came through Witchcraft, even though I had once "fought off" such homosexual advances while in college, and even though many Wiccan groups originally "doctrinally" opposed male homosexuality.

Willing to Do Anything

I remember a conversation I had with my long-suffering and very understanding wife in the midst of all this. I discussed with her the fact that I was pursuing a "Path of Wisdom." I told her I felt that if it could advance the course of esoteric Wisdom and give me greater comprehension of the mysteries of the Great Mother, I would be willing to do *anything* to acquire that initiatic wisdom.

In the course of that pursuit of "Wisdom," I got deeper into magical homosexuality and the strange alchemy of perversion. Tragically, I must confess that I began to enter groups where Nazi magick[26] and serious vampirism were practiced and child pornography was also being used and produced. Fortunately, about that time, the Lord began to bring me out of my spiritual "nose dive" into perdition.

Why was I so fortunate? That is something that can only be revealed in the innermost reaches of the depths of God's sovereign love. I only know that as I began to be drawn out of this garbage,

I watched friends, colleagues, and even initiators descend into realms of total madness. Alcoholism, prescription drug abuse and child pornography were moving through our circle of associates like the Black Death. Friends were disappearing into the mysterious subterranean world where sadism and sin reign supreme.

One of our prize "students" ended up utterly mad, even though she followed virtually the same steps and the same paths that we did. She began her path years before, as we had, seeking only the "gentle goddess." If Wicca is so innocent and so good, why do so many that *really* get into it in a deep way end up involved in perversion, crime and madness?

Many Witches, lacking any moral standard upon which to measure their sexual behavior would say the same thing I said, that they would do anything to move further on the path of Inner Wisdom. But they do not know where that path leads, and how difficult it becomes to overcome the magical momentum of evil they have set in motion once they have opened their bodies to obsessive uses not blessed by God.

Sexual perversion has been shown to be a more powerful addictive force than most drugs. This is because it opens these doorways through which spiritual beings of unimaginable rebellion and evil can enter and control your body and its impulses. It takes one of the greatest gifts that God has given us and twisted it into vile uses.

Is the "Sacred Altar" which the Wiccan Priesthood erects a sacrificial altar upon which the innocence and sanity of countless thousands of well-meaning people are immolated?

All these practices, aside from their connections with Crowley and his demonic mentor, Aiwass, are serious violations of the law of God. There are clear records, both within and without the Bible, which show that the practices of Paganism, both sexual and religious, lead to ever deeper forms of bondage, death and evil.

Have Witches been "infected" with this strain of demonic virus? If they are practicing their Craft seriously, they have, because they are calling upon false gods with talismans designs to invoke Set!

Jesus Christ brought me out of my moral tailspin before it was too late. Only through His cross and shed blood can the Witch be "inoculated" and cured of this kind of evil. But Jesus must be invited to work that healing, and He must be acknowledged as only true God and Savior!

Conclusion

Satan's Hoofprints
are All Over Wicca!

Even in the lower levels of Wicca, the doctrines of Satan begin to creep in. For our rite (the Alexandrian), the sign of Second Grade is the inverted pentagram drawn on the body.[1] This symbolizes the bottom seven **Sephirot** (or spheres) of the qabalistic Tree of Life.[2] Unfortunately it is also the symbol of the satanic Goat of Mendez, one of the most celebrated symbols of devil-worship.

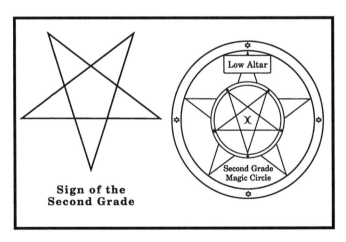

**Sign of the
Second Grade**

We were taught that this Grade was male (horned god) oriented, and that to invoke prosperity and power onto the earth plane, it was necessary to use this inverted pentagram. For us, the inverted star was the symbol of the god, and the upright star the symbol of the goddess. Thus, already in Second Grade, we were skating on the fringes of satanic practice.

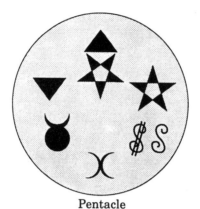

Pentacle

The "hoofprints" of Satan were all over Wicca, and they were literally on me! As a High Priest, I did one ceremony invoking my "higher self" or Holy Guardian Angel. The being who manifested caused a candle in the temple to erupt violently. A little ball of fire or hot wax (I'll never know for sure which) shot across the room and hit me in the forearm, leaving a searing brand in the precise shape of a cloven hoof. By that time, I saw it as a great blessing!

The question becomes, "How do you know that what you are doing is safe? How do you know that it isn't satanic, even in the lower degrees?

Even if you're just a witch and not a magician, are you still in grave danger?"[3]

Sadly, you are. Jesus tells us that anyone who is not with Him is against Him (Matthew 12:30). To be "with" Jesus means to accept Him as your Savior and make Him absolute Lord of your life. If you are a "white" witch, you probably either don't believe in Jesus at all, or you believe He was a great sage or wise man or adept, perhaps even a witch Himself. That is not the true Jesus!

Who Really Is Jesus?

Jesus is not a sage or adept, He is the Almighty Lord God of the Universe who came in the flesh, died and shed His blood for you. If you **aren't** trusting in **_that_** Jesus and **_that_** blood for **your** eternal destiny, then heartbreakingly, **you are** in Satan's camp.

You are part of a system of ritual which is ultimately controlled by Satan! It doesn't matter if you don't believe in Satan, he's still there and he's still horrifyingly real! Just because you don't believe in gravity doesn't mean that if you jump off a cliff you won't get splattered all over the landscape! The law of gravity cannot be violated with impunity, and neither can the laws of God.

If you think Satan is just a Christian myth, you are whistling in the dark. All you have to do is look over your shoulder and he is there, keeping his eye on his toy — YOU!

You don't have to be sacrificing virgins or turning crosses upside down to be a satanist! **All you have to do is spurn Jesus Christ and you are a satanist!** If you remember nothing else from this book, remember this:

ALL pagan religions are controlled by *Satan!*

It doesn't matter if you worship Pan or Krishna or Diana or Thor; the face behind the mask of your god is Satan's. Even if you are a purported atheist, you are still worshiping Satan; for you have undoubtedly made one element your idol (the center of your life): whether it's power, money, knowledge, freedom or some other ideal.

The true God says:

> I am the LORD thy God...Thou shalt have no other gods before me. Thou shalt not make unto thee any graven image (idol), or any likeness of any thing that is in heaven above, or that is in the earth beneath, or that is in the water under the earth: Thou shalt not bow down thyself to them, nor serve them: for I the LORD thy God am a jealous God...
> Exodus 20:2-5

It's that simple. There are *two* religious systems in the world. One is controlled by Satan. The other owes its only allegiance to Jesus Christ. Put simply, if you aren't a believer in Jesus Christ as Almighty God come in the flesh to save you from your sins, you *are* a satanist!

You see, both my wife and I worked unbelievably hard to be the best possible priestly couple we could be and lead our covens well. We studied and memorized rituals. We counselled our people and tried to help them with their various problems. We were desperately sincere, and thought Christianity was just a bigoted, monotheistic system of legalistic jive!

The Fantasy Goes Sour

But we were never really at peace. We did all the right things and tried to help our people grow, but they never seemed fulfilled either. They acted happy, but their eyes were dark and hollow. They said they were fulfilled, but their lives denied it. We were the ONLY married couple we knew in all our years of Wicca that didn't get divorced!

Sadly, a majority of the people we tried to help got worse! Many of them became either so filled with their own egos that they could never relate to anyone else or they sank into the mire of drugs or liquor. Two or three went quite insane!

In Milwaukee, we had psychic wars between groups. Witches were shooting at each other in the streets because of adultery! Curses were filling the air like mosquitoes on a hot Wisconsin night!

Pagans like to make fun of Catholics because of all the wars they started, but the only difference between the Pagans and the Catholics is that the Pagans never ran a government and had the power to raise armies. I used to read THE GREEN EGG, Tim Zell's Neo-pagan magazine. Almost every issue contained a vicious feud in the letter columns.

Why? Because you are dealing with sinful, fallen human beings, that's why! God says the human heart is desperately wicked and deceitful above all things (Jeremiah 17:9). Without Jesus Christ, people are going to act like spoiled brats! Look around you! How else can you account for all the evil in the world? Killing, bigotry, rape and war — these are the fruits of Satan-worship, under its many guises.

But love, joy, peace, patience, and long-suffering are the fruits of the Holy Spirit.

You may not call yourself a satanist, but if you have not made Jesus Christ your Lord and Master, then Satan is your lord and master. We learned this the hard way! No amount of effort, study or practice on your part will ever bring you the peace or fulfillment you seek. Nor will belonging to any church, Protestant, Catholic or Jewish.

If I'm a Witch, What Can I Do?

Christianity is not a religion! It is anti-religion!! Religion is man's attempts to do certain things to please his deity. Christianity is a relationship with the Lord of the Universe, Jesus Christ!

Only trusting in Jesus for your salvation can make you a saved person:

> For whosoever shall call upon the name of the Lord shall be saved. Romans 10:13

Church affiliation or following a litany of legalistic rules won't do it. Those concepts are lies foisted on the world by Satan, then gradually adopted by many major denominations. But it is not what the Bible says:

> That if thou shalt confess with thy mouth the Lord Jesus, and shalt believe in thine heart that God hath raised him from the dead, thou shalt be saved. For with the heart man believeth unto righteousness; and with the mouth confession is made unto salvation.
> Romans 10:9-10

Religionists, of whatever stripe, who make a career out of frightening people and making them work their way to God, are preaching a lie from the pit of hell! You don't have to live your life in agony, wondering about your fate after death. Nor do you have to worry about "karma" and the wheel of rebirth! John the Apostle wrote:

> These things have I written unto you that believe on the name of the Son of God; that ye may **_know_** that ye have eternal life. 1 John 5:13

Not hope, but "KNOW" that you can have

eternal life with God forever! Consider the alternative Wicca offers you, supposedly lifetime after lifetime trying to pick up your mistakes from previous lifetimes.[4] I would not treat a DOG that badly!

Besides, isn't the prospect of living in resurrected glory with Jesus more appealing than spending a few more hundred lifetimes running around the treadmill of the wheel of karma, chasing a shapeless future?

Jesus makes it so easy for you. All you have to do is lay aside your pride and belief in all those Pagan gods and admit that they cannot save you. Ask Jesus to forgive your sins and save you from hell and to be the Lord of your life (Romans 10:9-13). Jesus is real, and will be delighted to meet you right where you are!

Thank God, there is an alternative — a blessed assurance of eternal life! That's quite a promise! All you need to do to receive it is simply do these five things:

1. Admit to God that you're not perfect, that you're a sinner. As the Bible says: "For all have sinned, and come short of the glory of God." (Romans 3:23). Realize that it is only by having faith in Jesus and Him only for your salvation that you can become a child of God and heir to the promise. (Ephesians 2:8-9).

2. Repent and turn away from those sins, especially the sin of witchcraft. God says,

"...rebellion is as the sin of witchcraft;" (1 Samuel 15:23) and "Except ye repent, ye shall all likewise perish." (Luke 13:3).

3. Pray and ask Jesus to come into your heart and take away your sins! (Romans 10:9-13). Ask Him to be your Savior! "For there is one God, and one mediator between God and men, the man Christ Jesus." (1 Timothy 2:5)

4. Make Jesus the Lord of your life and give Him control over every part of it. See John 14:15: "If ye love me, keep my commandments." And Romans 12:1-2:

> "I beseech you therefore, brethren, by the mercies of God, that ye present your bodies a living sacrifice, holy, acceptable unto God, which is your reasonable service. And be not conformed to this world: but be ye transformed by the renewing of your mind, that ye may prove what is that good, and acceptable, and perfect will of God."

5. Then know that you are saved (1 John 5:13) and that Satan no longer has any hold over you. You have full assurance of heaven — assurance that no person can give, but Jesus can! He said, "I am the way, the truth, and the life: no man cometh unto the Father, but by me." (John 14:6)

It's that simple! Why put your trust in books and rituals that were written by flawed men and women — especially since much of it is manufactured and made up out of whole cloth?

Are people like Alex Sanders or Gerald Gardner worth trusting over Jesus? Who else can redeem you?

If you say, as some "white" witches have to me, that you need no redeemer — that you depend on yourself for spiritual salvation; then you are mouthing the creeds of the satanist! Anton LaVey, the head of the Church of Satan, wrote:

> Here and now is our day of joy! Here and now is our opportunity! Choose ye this day, this hour, for no redeemer liveth. Say unto thine own heart, *I am mine own redeemer.*[5]

You see how far into the enemy's camp you already are? You are telling Jesus Christ that you don't need Him! You are saying to Him that He shed His blood on Calvary in vain in your case! Why do you ignore the plain testimony of His resurrection and saving power? Why do you ignore the Bible in favor of religions made up by people? Why do you trust Gerald Gardner more than the most trustworthy book in human history?

God has promised that His Word (Who is Jesus, see John 1:1-14) will endure forever! His Word is perfect and eternal and will outlast both the heavens and the earth (Matt.5:18; 1 Peter 1:24-25) Can't you take Him at His word?

Realize, as I did after over a year of study and research, that not one Biblical prophecy has failed to happen exactly as predicted; and that

Jesus Himself was the fulfillment of over 300 Old Testament prophecies! Some prophecies in Daniel foretold events hundreds and even thousands of years in the future, yet all have been fulfilled right down to the very year! What witch or psychic has that kind of track record?

Please remember, we're talking about eternity here! What if your belief system is wrong — dangerously wrong? God says that without Jesus, you, as a Witch or Pagan, will go into the lake of fire (Revelation 21:8). Are the books and people in whom you are putting your faith for spiritual success *that* trustworthy? Don't you owe it to yourself to at least investigate what I'm telling you?

Remember, I've been there! Wicca, however noble and idealistic it might seem, is a modern, artificial religion created by cleaning up continental satanism a bit. It's like putting rouge and mascara on a decomposing corpse! The rotten, putrid heart is the same, it just looks nicer.

There are only two kinds of Wiccans, the "higher ups" who know that Satan is their god; and the innocent ones of lower Grade who think they're worshipping nature deities.

Which kind are you?

In case you have any thoughts about trying to remain an "innocent" Pagan, just playing in the forest and worshiping the goddess, hear what

God's Word has to say about nature deities:

> Professing themselves to be wise (wise ones?), they became fools, And changed the glory of the uncorruptible God into an image made like to corruptible man, and to birds, and fourfooted beasts, and creeping things. Wherefore God also gave them up to uncleanness through the lusts of their own hearts, to dishonour their own bodies between themselves: Who changed the truth of God into a lie, and worshipped and served the creature more than the Creator, who is blessed forever. Amen.
>
> Romans 1:22-25

Come to Jesus! It will be the best decision you ever made!

If you feel you need more information about this, you can write us:

Bill and Sharon Schnoebelen
With One Accord Ministries
P.O. Box 457
Dubuque, IA 52004-0457

E-mail address: withone@netins.net

Footnotes

Introduction

1. Wicca, pronounced "Wicha," contrary to popular practice, is the term most witches prefer to use for their faith. They pronounce it "Wikka" and frequently assert that it means "Wise One."
2. Margaret Murray's books, THE WITCH CULT IN WESTERN EUROPE and THE GOD OF THE WITCHES, did much to popularize the concept that Wicca is a survival of ancient religions. In recent years, though, their scholarship has been seriously challenged.
3. See Margot Adler's DRAWING DOWN THE MOON, Beacon Press, Boston, 1986 rev. ed., p.46.
4. Adler, p. 11.
5. Ibid. p.10.

Chapter 1

1. Many witches and ceremonial magicians spell magic with a "k" to distinguish it from stage magic or illusion. Our groups followed this practice, apparently begun by early 20th century satanist Aleister Crowley.
2. See Francis King's RITUAL MAGIC IN ENGLAND, especially the chapter "A Whip for Aradia." Also Elliot Rose's A RAZOR FOR A GOAT, U. of Toronto Press, Toronto, 1962, especially p.3, 8-10, 40, and 218.
3. Doreen Valiente, WITCHCRAFT FOR TOMORROW, Phoenix Publishing, Custer, WA., 1978, rev. 1987, p.13.
4. Adler, p.81.
5. Ibid., p.69 for a presentation of this kind of argument.
6. Crowley was a satanic genius of the first order. He rebelled against his fundamentalist upbringing and joined the Rosicrucian/Masonic society, The Golden Dawn. Magic has never been the same since. Crowley claimed that a superhuman being, Aiwas, communicated to him a book called LIBER AL VEL LEGIS (the Book of the Law) which was to abrogate the Bible. Crowley blasphemed Jesus and the Biblical God, and tried to found a new religion called Crowleyanity or THELEMA (from the Greek word for "will"). This came from the cardinal doctrine of his religion: "Do what thou wilt shall be the whole of the law. Love is the law, love under will." He died a miserable heroin addict in 1947, having produced volumes of brilliant but obscene rituals and poetry.
7. Valiente, p.21.
8. Francis King, THE RITES OF MODERN OCCULT MAGIC, MacMillan, N.Y., 1970, pp.176, 179-80.
9. Adler, p.64.
10. "The Book of the Law," a 3-chapter prose-poem supposedly received by Crowley through trance communication in 1904, claims to be the destruction of Christianity and the coming forth of the New Age of the

Crowned and Conquering Child, the Egyptian war-god, Horus. It has been a very influential volume in 20th century magic and satanism.

11. Adler, p.85.
12. See Janet and Stewart Farrar, THE WITCHES' GODDESS, Phoenix Publishing, 1987, p.57.
13. Jung's concepts, especially the archetype, have become essential to modern Neo-paganism. His extensive writings have provided much of the philosophical underpinning for modern occultism. Unfortunately, Jung's teachings have also had a powerful influence on the Christian church. Through such influential writers as Morton Kelsey and Agnes Sanford, many of Jung's occult ideas have become part of evangelical Christianity, especially in the charismatic movement and in counseling.
14. "Rede" is an old English word for rule. The Wiccan Rede is like the "Golden Rule" of Wiccan ethics. In addition to its resemblance to Crowley's dictum, it sounds suspiciously like the situational ethics of the hippie movement and on, even into the 1980's.
15. This is Third Grade in Gardnerian Wicca.
16. For a complete account of this ritual drama, see Stewart Farrar's WHAT WITCHES DO, Coward, McCann & Geoghegan, New York, 1971, pp.195-96.
17. A shaman is a witch-doctor in primitive societies. Many modern philosophers of occultism speak of the witch's growth as developing into a shaman, a "walker between the worlds" of spirit and reality, good and evil.
18. Miriam Starhawk, DREAMING THE DARK: THE SPIRAL JOURNEY: A REBIRTH OF THE ANCIENT RELIGION OF THE GREAT GODDESS, Doubleday, New York, 1979, p.19.
19. Ralph Metzner, "Owning our Shadow: Recognizing and Accepting the Enemy Within," NEW REALITIES, Jan/Feb 1987, pp.34-37, cited in Texe Marrs' MYSTERY MARK OF THE NEW AGE, Crossways Books, 1988, p.218.
20. Matthew Fox, ORIGINAL BLESSING, Bear & Co., 1983, Santa Fe, NM, p.137.
21. Ibid., p.162.
22. Marrs, p.216.
23. Ibid., p.205.
24. Adepthood is 5th degree in magick, and is a major step beyond classical Wicca into the realms of ceremonial magick. An adept can have dialog with his higher self or god-self.
25. See Farrar and Farrar, 1987, p.39, 163-4 for an example of how central the name Lucifer is in classic Wicca.
26. A popular book on THE CHURCH OF ALL WORLDS reading list was Robert Graves' KING JESUS, a novel which claimed that Jesus and Mary Magdelene (who was supposedly a High Priestess of the Great Mother) came together to fuse the traditions of Judaism and Wicca.

It was taken seriously by many of us as an important poetic/psychic insight into Jesus.

27. This is a common theme in the New Age movement today, and has been answered by several excellent writers. See footnote 43 for brief bibliography. Also THE MYSTICAL MAZE by Pat Means, Campus Crusade for Christ, 1976; and GODS OF THE NEW AGE by Caryl Matrisciana, Harvest House, 1985; and THE BEAUTIFUL SIDE OF EVIL by Johanna Michaelsen, Harvest House, 1984.

28. Anton Szandor LaVey, THE SATANIC BIBLE, Avon Books, New York, 1969, p.272.

29. In spite of frequent disclaimers from "white" witches concerning the practice of animal sacrifice, consummate white Wiccan author Doreen Valiente comes up with precisely the same ethical analysis for killing animals in Tantra ritual in her book, op.cit., p.24

30. This old lie, that certain occult beliefs like reincarnation were censored out of the Bible and the early church by the Council of Constantinople, has received new popularity due to Shirley MacLaine's TV miniseries. This was also used by supposed Wiccan scholar Doreen Valiente in 1978, op.cit., p.39. This belongs to the "If you tell a lie often enough, it becomes the truth" school of history.

31. Sybil Leek, DIARY OF A WITCH, Prentice-Hall, 1968, pp.17-19.

32. See Doreen Valiente, AN ABC OF WITCHCRAFT, New York, St.Martin's Press, 1973, pp.155-57. She also notes passages in the BOOK OF SHADOWS from Ovid, Rudyard Kipling, C.G. Leland, Crowley and the ceremonial magick text, THE KEY OF SOLOMON!! See also Farrar, p.93 (and note). Also Janet & Stewart Farrar, EIGHT SABBATS FOR WITCHES, Robert Hale, London, 1981, pp.41-42, 47, 52.

33. See Maury Terry's THE ULTIMATE EVIL: AN INVESTIGATION OF AMERICA'S MOST DANGEROUS SATANIC CULT, Dolphin Doubleday, Garden City, NY, 1987, p.485-86.

34. Farrar, p.191.

35. Ibid. p.41, and Johns, p.9.

36. Adler, p.101.

37. Farrar, p.202 and Farrar and Farrar, p.175.

38. Most think a warlock is just a male witch, but few Wiccans use the term that way. Its root is an Anglo-Saxon word meaning "traitor" or "deceiver." Since Wiccans are so concerned about their "nice" image, they have dropped the word from use. LaVey, however, had no such compunctions and shamelessly restored the title to his second degree male witches.

39. Farrar & Farrar, p. 42 (note) and Johns, pp.15 and 17.

40. Johns, pp.148-49.

41. It may sound strange to call the Church of Satan innocuous, but compared to real satanic cults it definitely is. LaVey does not permit either animal or human sacrifice and discourages the use of drugs, all things that are mainstays of hard-core satanism. His brand of

satanism is little more than a blend of Ayn Rand's philosophy of Objectivism (radical selfishness) and gothic satanic trappings.

42. Adler, p. 11.
43. Ibid. p.10.

Chapter 2

1. Quoted from Witches' League for Public Awareness tract, 1988.
2. This scourging is done with a small ceremonial whip made of cords. It is done harder in Second degree than in First degree. In the A/G Wiccan traditions, it can often raise small welts, but it isn't usually as bad as it sounds. The severity of the scourging is up to the High Priestess, and some of them whip pretty hard, teaching the candidate that they must "suffer in order to learn."
3. A rope is passed around the neck, then used to secure hands behind back. The knees and ankles are both tied together.
4. From a non-published Book of Shadows of the Alexandrian rite in possession of the author, p.32. Also found in published form in THE GRIMOIRE OF LADY SHEBA, Llewellyn, St. Paul, MN., 1974, p.135.
5. Realize that the term "vendetta" came from the Sicilian occult society, the Mafia, and that it is based on the same principles of Sicilian witchcraft (stregoi) as this Three-fold law is in Anglo-Saxon Wicca.
6. Janet & Stewart Farrar, THE WITCHES' GODDESS, Phoenix, 1987, p.163 relates much of the celebrated "Gospel of the Witches," and the name of the god of the witches as Lucifer, the Goddess Diana's brother and lover, and the father of Aradia, the bringer of witchcraft to earth.
7. THE RANDOM HOUSE DICTIONARY OF THE ENGLISH LANGUAGE, second edition, unabridged, pp.2142-2143.
8. THE COMPACT EDITION OF THE OXFORD ENGLISH DICTIONARY, (1971 edition) vol.2, p.3688.
9. Ibid.
10. Book of Shadows, p.52-53.
11. Cf. many issues of the early Neo-Pagan Newsletter, The Green Egg, for advertisements of the Warlock Shoppe and the subsequent controversy over the use of the name. It still exists under its new name, The Magickal Chylde, at 35 W. 19th St., Manhattan, N.Y.

Chapter 3

1. Recently re-released as THE SATANIC WITCH, Feral House, Los Angeles, 1989.
2. This term seems to have first been used by author Robert Burton in his philosophical treatise, THE ANATOMY OF MELACHOLY, written in 1621.
3. The WLPA, which is one of the most nervy attempts at revisionism in modern memory, is headed up by Gov. Michael Dukakis' official witch

of Massassachusetts, Laurie Cabot, with headquarters at Box 8736, Salem, MA. 01971-8736.

4. RANDOM HOUSE. pp.2172 and 2182.
5. OXFORD, p.3797.
6. Anton LaVey,THE SATANIC RITUALS,University Books, N.Y.1972, p.13
7. RANDOM HOUSE, p.2182.
8. WEBSTER'S NEW WORLD DICTIONARY, Third College ed., p.1534.
9. AMERICAN HERITAGE DICTIONARY, Second College ed., p.1386.
10. Bob Larson, SATANISM: THE SEDUCTION OF AMERICA'S YOUTH, Thomas Nelson, 1989, p.180.

Chapter 4

1. Though a full examination of these denials is beyond the scope of this book, the Roman church denies the finished work of Jesus' sacrifice on Calvary, salvation by faith alone, the unique Mediatorship of Jesus and the all-sufficiency of the Bible as our source of divine truth. See also ROMAN CATHOLICISM, by Lorraine Boettner (P&R Publishing).
2. Aleister Crowley and Alex Sanders, to name a couple.
3. A voodoo goddess of love and the sea.
4. Catholics offer prayers for the dead, to get them out of Purgatory. Witches believe in communicating with the dead, especially at Samhain; and that they can, through mediumship, help lower level spirits achieve higher areas of growth before they incarnate again.
5. Although this self-mortification element has been toned down recently in U.S. Catholicism, wearing of hair shirts, barbed wire corsets and self-flagellation (whipping) were regularly practiced within Catholic monasteries and nunneries until at least the 1960's. It may still be going on today in the U.S. and is definitely still practiced overseas. Witches believe you must be willing to "suffer in order to learn" and most practice at least ceremonial whipping of each other. Wiccan authors also brag about how they whipped each other into a magical frenzy in order to raise a large enough "cone of power" to turn back both the Spanish Armada and the forces of Hitler.
6. cf. FOXE'S BOOK OF MARTYRS (1805 edition) for many accounts of Bible-Believers who were tortured and slain by the Inquisition.
7. See Mt. 5:24, 18:15; Luke 17:3; Rom. 14:1, 15:1; II Cor. 2:6; Gal. 6:1 and I Thess. 5:14 for counsel on dealing with unbelievers and heretics.
8. The word literally means "Law of God" Theo-nomos, and is repre-sented by several writers in Christianity like Rushdoony and North. Both groups are on the fringe of Christian orthodoxy.
9. Hitler was not a Christian, but a loyal son of the Catholic church. (See THE UNKNOWN HITLER by Wulf Schwarzwaller, Berkeley Books, New York, 1989, pp.101-102, 107; ADOLPH HITLER by John Toland, (Doubleday, New York, 1976, vol. 2, p. 803; THE NAZI PERSECUTION OF THE CHURCHES, 1933-45 by J. S. Conway, Basic Books, New York, 1968, pp. 24-26.

Chapter 5

1. Not bugs, but spiritual parasites, believed to control and possess undefended people, almost like demons. Some witches believe in demons or evil spirits and others do not. Those who believe in their existence do not view them as Christians do, but rather see them as low-level astral plane riff-raff that any witch worth her salt can kick out with a wave of her athame! In "white witchcraft" circles, they are not believed to be beings of any great threat, but more like spiritual lice. An irritation, but never very dangerous. Only in the higher levels of magic do you encounter a belief in villainous and potent demons.

2. This is a Hindu term, "chakra" meaning "wheel." It is like a spiritual or astral ganglion (or bundle) of energy. Classic occult thought teaches that there are seven such chakras running up and down your spine, beginning with one in your tailbone or anus and ending with your "Crown" chakra.

3. From a private copy of the Alexandrian rite Book of Shadows in possession of the author, p.53.

4. RANDOM HOUSE DICTIONARY, unabridged, p.891.

5. Book of Shadows, pp.40-41.

6. THE GRIMOIRE OF LADY SHEBA, Llewellyn Publications, St. Paul, MN., 1974, p.9.

7. Ibid., p.87.

8. Ibid.

9. Shamanism has now become fashionable, and is a major buzz-word in New Age groups today (cf. The Way of the Shaman). Basically, a shaman is a witch doctor, an occult priest or priestess who can move between dream states and different levels of reality at will through the use of drugs, meditations and magic rites.

Chapter 6

1. Margot Adler, DRAWING DOWN THE MOON, (revised edition) 1986, p.112.

2. From the Charge of the Goddess in the "Drawing Down the Moon" ceremony in the Book of Shadows, quoted in Stewart Farrar's WHAT WITCHES DO, Coward, McCann, & Geoghegan, New York, 1971, p.21.

3. August 16, 1985, Los Angeles Herald Examiner.

4. Alexander Eliot, Mircea Eliade, Joseph Campbell, MYTHS, McGraw-Hill, New York, 1976, p.44,

5. Janet & Stewart Farrar, THE WITCHES' GODDESS, Phoenix, 1987, p.130-131.

6. Lewis Spence, AN ENCYLCOPEDIA OF OCCULTISM, Citadel Book, Secaucus, N. J. 1977, p.251

7. "Child Sacrifice at Carthage and in the Bible," Biblical Archaelogical Review, January/February 1984.

8. Nigel Davis, HUMAN SACRIFICE IN HISTORY AND TODAY, p.59.
9. M. Esther Harding, WOMAN'S MYSTERIES—ANCIENT AND MODERN, Harper & Row, 1971, p.138.
10. Ibid.
11. The name comes from the belief that the climax of the ceremony is the possession of the coven's High Priestess by the Goddess herself. The moon goddess is "drawn down" into her body.
12. Farrar & Farrar, op.cit., p.64 asserts that the Charge was adapted by Gerald Gardner from old Tuscan witch rituals and then revised by Doreen Valiente with his approval.
13. From the Book of Shadows, quoted in Farrar, op.cit., p.197.
14. Ibid., p.198.
15. Alex Sanders Lectures on Witchcraft (J.W. Baker, editor), Lecture 3, "The Eight Working Tools of the Wicca," last paragraph (no page numbers)
16. See June Johns, KING OF THE WITCHES, Coward-McCann, 1969, p.15.
17. RANDOM HOUSE DICTIONARY, unabridged 2nd edition, p.122.
18. Frederick Adams' Feraferia group was organized into groves rather than covens.

Chapter 7
1. In 1 Chronicles 21:1; Job 1 & 2; Ps. 109:6 and Zechariah 3:1-2.
2. Thompson Chain Reference Bible, fourth Edition, Indianapolis, IN p.513
3. Kerubim are the angels shown kneeling over the celebrated Ark of the Covenant, and are quite mysterious and powerful beings. Contrary to popular art, they are not chubby little naked babies with wings, bows and arrows.
4. THE NEW YORK PUBLIC LIBRARY DESK REFERENCE, Simon & Schuster, 1989, p.196.
5. This may be why the New Age movement, which is Monism, is so popular among "Yuppies" and celebrities like Shirley MacLaine and Linda Evans. These people often live in fantasy existences, divorced from much of the daily grind and tragedy in life. They are the U.S. equivalent of the upper castes in India.
6. Statistics in this paragraph from DESK REFERENCE, op.cit. pp.189-191.
7. Kenneth Grant, THE MAGICAL REVIVAL, Samuel Weiser, 1973, p.61.
8. Ibid., p.65.
9. E.A. Wallis Budge, THE EGYPTIAN BOOK OF THE DEAD, Dover, New York, 1977, Chapter 175.
10. Albert Churchward, THE ORIGIN AND EVOLUTION OF RELIGION, p. 189.
11. Alexander Eliot, Mircea Eliade & Joseph Campbell, MYTHS, McGraw-Hill, 1976, pp. 156, 258.

Chapter 8

1. Another term borrowed from Hinduism. Akasha is the phantom stuff of the astral plane. It is the primordial energy web which holds the universe together. Thus, everything anyone does is imprinted upon the Akasha, like having your picture recorded on film. The cumulative record of one's lives are thus recorded somewhere on the Akasha. This is called the Akashic record. Supposedly, sensitives like psychics or mediums can "read" this record and tell you things about your past lives. Of course, there is never any way of telling if they are right or not. This makes Akashic readings one of the most popular functions of mediums and psychics, since they can say just about anything (the more outlandish the better) and never be caught in a false prophecy. Convenient.
2. By Dr. Ian Stevenson.
3. Ibid., p.377.
4. The best known being Elizabeth Clare Prophet's Church Universal and Triumphant (or Summit Lighthouse) which tries to blend Hinduism, Catholicism, Right-wing politics and New Age philosophy into an unholy stew more dangerous than the sum of its individual parts.
5. John Snyder, REINCARNATION VS. RESURRECTION, Moody Press,1984. Also Caryl Matrisiciana GODS OF THE NEW AGE, Harvest House, 1985, and F. LaGard Smith, OUT ON A BROKEN LIMB, Harvest House, 1986.

Chapter 9

1. THE FOURTH BOOK OF AGRIPPA, a classic grimoire, p.123-124 recommends the use of blood to animate a corpse. Homer was familiar with this practice in 800 B.C. and his work, THE ODYSSEY, contains an episode of using blood to animate the shades of the dead; cf. E.O. James, ORIGINS OF SACRIFICE.
2. Francis Barrett, THE MAGUS, 1801 reprint, University Books, 1967, Book II, part 1, p.69.
3. Arthur Edward Waite, BOOK OF CEREMONIAL MAGIC, 1961, p.324; also Reginald Scot's A DISCOURSE CONCERNING DEVILS AND SPIRITS, p.67 published in the 16th century.
4. Paul Huson, MASTERING WITCHCRAFT, G.P. Putnam's Sons, 1970, p.156.
5. Janet & Stewart Farrar, EIGHT SABBATS FOR WITCHES, 1981, p.122. Lewis Spence, THE HISTORY AND ORIGINS OF DRUIDISM, 1976, p.104.
6. THE GRIMOIRE OF LADY SHEBA, Llewellyn, 1974, p.129.
7. Ibid.
8. Ibid.
9. Huson, p.53 alludes to this practice.
10. Margaret A. Murray, THE GOD OF THE WITCHES, Oxford University

press, 1931, 1970, p.160-161.

11. The legend of King Arthur and Guinevere and Lancelot is steeped in Witchcraft and Paganism, which has been thinly disguised in modern versions. See feminist science fiction writer Marion Zimmer Bradley's book, THE MISTS OF AVALON, for a more Paganized retelling of the legend.

12. Perhaps the best known book on this is Jessie L. Weston's FROM RITUAL TO ROMANCE, Cambridge Press.

13. Sir James George Frazer, THE GOLDEN BOUGH, MacMillan, abridged edition,1922, 1950, esp. pp.376-410, 308-319.

14. Rev. Alexander Hislop, THE TWO BABYLONS, Loizeux Brothers, Neptune, N.J., 1959 (first ed. 1916), pp.55-58

15. Murray, op.cit.pp.167-197.

16. Ibid., pp.122-124.

17. As may be guessed, the exceptions are semen and Bartholin fluid.

18. Frazer, op.cit., p.308.

19. Please understand: contrary to the teachings of the Jehovah's Witness cult, this teaching has nothing to do with blood transfusions.

20. Acts 15:29.

21. 2 Kings 23:10, Jeremiah 32:35

22. The 8 sun-oriented rituals of the Wicca are called sabbats, and often involve invoking the Horned God rather than the Goddess.

23. Genesis 3:21.

24. Leviticus 1:3, 3:1-6, 4:28, etc.

25. Hebrews 10:11

Chapter 10

1. June Johns, KING OF THE WITCHES, Coward McCann, New York, 1969, p.151.

2. Perfect couples are usually working partners who are "handfasted" together, but not legally married; hence they amount to a kind of common law Wiccan marriage.

3. Stewart Farrar, WHAT WITCHES DO, Coward McCann & Geoghegan, 1971, p.189-190.

4. Gavin & Yvonne Frost, THE WITCH'S BIBLE, Nash Publications, 1972, p.84.

5. Frost, pp.83-90.

6. Ibid. pp.85-86.

7. Ibid. 70-71.

8. Doreen Valiente, NATURAL MAGIC, St Martin's, 1975, p.86ff.

9. Kenneth Grant, THE MAGICAL REVIVAL, Samuel Weiser,1973,p121-122

10. Valiente, p.90-91.

11. Kenneth Grant, NIGHTSIDE OF EDEN, Frederick Muller, Ltd., 1977, p.69.

12. Kenneth Grant, ALEISTER CROWLY AND THE HIDDEN GOD, Samuel Weiser, 1974, p.12.

13. Grant, REVIVAL, p.61
14. "Thelema" means "will" in Greek, and it applies here to the Crowlean maxim of "Do what thou wilt." The Book of the Law is believed by many Witches and occultists to be one of the definitive divine revelations of this century, and for the New Age.
15. Liber AL vel Legis, sub figura CCXX, as quoted in THE EQUINOX OF THE GODS, by Aleister Crowley, privately published by the O.T.O., 1936; 1:40 (p.18)
16. See Aleister Crowley, THE EQUINOX, vol.3, no.1, Samuel Weiser, 1973, pp.247-270 for the complete ritual of the Gnostic Mass.
17. Farrar, op.cit, p.94.
18. Crowley, EQUINOX, p.258 contains essentially the same invocation.
19. Grant, NIGHTSIDE, p.136.
20. Ibid. pp.143-255
21. Grant, REVIVAL, p.94, note.
22. Ibid., p.131-133.
23. See Schnoebelen and Spencer, MORMONISM'S TEMPLE OF DOOM, Triple J Publications, 1987, p. 44 for a brief explanation of the Tree of Life's symbolism and place of importance in Western occultism.
24. See Mantak Chia & Michael Winn, TAOIST SECRETS OF LOVE, Aurora Press, 1984, p.116.
25. Grant, REVIVAL, p.74.
26. For examples of satanist rite drawn from the "Nazi current," see THE SATANIC RITUALS by Anton LaVey, University Books, 1972, Das Tierdrama, and Die Elektrischen Vorspiel, pp.76-130. LaVey's pupil, Dr. Michael Aquino, now head of the Temple of Set, in October, 1984, also invoked the forces of Nazi magic in the bombed out ruins of the castle in Germany where the SS rituals were done.

Conclusion

1. Farrar, p.57 and 88 for data on inverted pentagams that is available to non-witches.
2. See author's forthcoming book for an explanation of the Tree of Life and the Qabalah's relationship to magick.
3. There is a difference between a witch and a magician. Witches worship the gods. Magicians try to command and conquer them, and believe they can become gods themselves. In the Alexandrian rite we got into magick and hermetics in the higher degrees. Many Wicca groups don't.
4. See the chapter on reincarnation. Also see REINCARNATION VS. RESURRECTION by John Snyder, Moody Press, Chicago, 1984. Also UNMASKING THE NEW AGE by Douglas R. Groothuis, Intervarsity Press, Downers Grove, Il., 1986; and OUT ON A BROKEN LIMB by F. LaGard Smith, Harvest House, Eugene, OR., 1986.
5. LaVey, pg. 33